150 BEST TINY SPACE IDEAS

150 BEST TINY SPACE IDEAS

FRANCESC ZAMORA MOLA

HARPER
DESIGN

An Imprint of Harper Collins Publishers

First published in 2019 by:
Harper Design
An Imprint of HarperCollins*Publishers*
195 Broadway
New York, NY 10007
Tel.: (212) 207-7000
Fax: (855) 746-6023
harperdesign@harpercollins.com
www.hc.com

Distributed throughout the world by:
HarperCollins*Publishers*
195 Broadway
New York, NY 10007

Editorial coordinator: Claudia Martínez Alonso
Art director: Mireia Casanovas Soley
Editor and texts: Francesc Zamora Mola
Layout: Cristina Simó Perales

ISBN 978-0-06-290922-0

Library of Congress Control Number: 2016958633

Printed in China
First printing, 2019

CONTENTS

Introduction

The tiny spaces included in this book range between 140 and 500 square feet in size. They are set in urban and in rural contexts. The ones in urban settings support a lifestyle that enjoys the proximity of city amenities and promote the building of communities in the heart of cities. Those set in natural settings tend to satisfy the desire for simple living away from the chaos of cities, the overstimulation of the senses, and the forces that disconnect people from meaningful values. With ideas that seem so disparate, the two types have emerged from the Tiny House Movement.

The Tiny House Movement is a global architectural and social movement that advocates living a simpler life in small spaces and has been a clarion call to address the shortage of space and affordable housing in urban areas. City authorities are rewriting zoning codes to encourage density and promote creative uses of tiny spaces such as ADUs (accessory dwelling units) and micro-apartments. The development of such living spaces might be a way to provide affordable housing to a generation of city dwellers who are more interested in living a city lifestyle than in the prospect of owning a large house with a two-car garage.

The average size of a tiny home is around 300 square feet, which is roughly the size of a one-car garage. Does this sound cramped? The examples shown in this book prove otherwise.

Graham Hill, owner and founder of LifeEdited, a design and development firm that created LE2 (pages 20-29), observes that "we intuitively desire simpler lives filled with high-quality experiences, relationships, and possessions. The smaller size makes life more manageable." The nature of the way we live is changing at the rhythm demographics change. These changes will keep bringing with them interesting uses of space, particularly in dense urban communities. Michael Chen of Michael K Chen

Architecture (see Attic Transformer, pages 144-155), says that "as cities become denser, an inventive approach to design for smaller spaces is becoming ever more important to the pursuit of a well-lived urban life."

At the same time, the force that drives urbanites to downsize and focus on a lifestyle of quality also challenges people to think about buildings in the landscape from every angle, from construction to environmental impact. According to Rupert McKelvie of British design firm Out of the Valley (see Oak Cabin, pages 306-313), "the popularity of small, simple dwellings reflects the need for escapism felt by many people who lead busy lives in cities. Cabins offer a space that allows their occupants to live more modestly and reconnect with simple pleasures."

Regardless of location, whether in the city or in the wild, the Tiny House Movement has been encouraging creative designs. Multifunctional furniture is often the key to making tiny spaces work. As exercises in minimal living, some of the projects included in the book achieve an extraordinary level of spatial clarity, while others display elements of complex multifunctionality. New technology has contributed greatly to the success of space-saving solutions, including convertible furniture and sliding walls that transform spaces according to different needs. The stunning solutions make tiny spaces highly desirable dwellings and demonstrate that living small doesn't require giving up on comfort.

The Tiny House Movement has received wide media coverage with shows such as *Tiny House Nation*. In the show, the hosts travel the North American territory in search of small dwellings and their creative owners.

The undisputable popularity of tiny living spaces continues to grow, paving the path for other forms of habitations, such as co-living, as the demographics relentlessly change.

Tiny Apartments

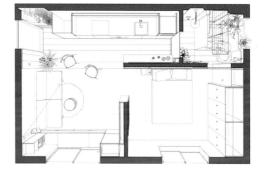

Carmel Place is the result of "MY MICRO NY," a winning entry by Brooklyn-based nARCHITECTS and Monadnock Development in the city's 2012 adAPT NYC competition. This initiative was launched as part of former Mayor Bloomberg's administration's New Housing Marketplace Plan to accommodate the city's growing small-household population. Carmel Place is one of the first micro-unit apartment buildings in New York City and also one of the first multiunit buildings to use modular construction. Its construction consisted of the fabrication, transportation, and stacking of sixty-five individual self-supporting steel-framed modules, fifty-five of which serve as residential micro-units while the remaining ten serve as the building's core.

Carmel Place

260–360 sq ft

nARCHITECTS

New York City, New York,
United States

© Iwan Baan and Pablo Enriquez,
courtesy nARCHITECTS

Our Community
1 borough, 1 neighborhood,
1 street,
1 Mount Carmel Place

Our Micro Towers
55 units, 4 towers,
10 floors,
1 community

Our Shared Spaces
3,525 sq ft exterior space,
5,470 sq ft interior amenities,
1 key card

Our Micro Modules
65 modules,
5 weeks to erect them

My Micro Unit
Average 286 sq ft,
2 zones,
1 home

Nested scales of Carmel Place diagram

Percent of single-person households nationwide

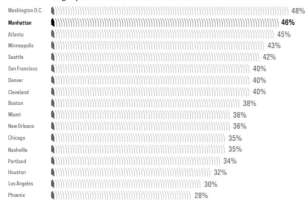

Washington D.C.	48%
Manhattan	**46%**
Atlanta	45%
Minneapolis	43%
Seattle	42%
San Francisco	40%
Denver	40%
Cleveland	40%
Boston	38%
Miami	36%
New Orleans	36%
Chicago	35%
Nashville	35%
Portland	34%
Houston	32%
Los Angeles	30%
Phoenix	28%

Percent of single-person households worldwide

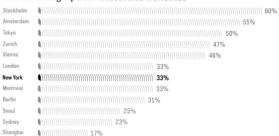

Stockholm	60%
Amsterdam	55%
Tokyo	50%
Zurich	47%
Vienna	46%
London	33%
New York	**33%**
Montreal	33%
Berlin	31%
Seoul	25%
Sydney	23%
Shanghai	17%

Conceived as a microcosm of the city skyline, the building has four slender "mini towers" that adapt the concept of micro-living to the form and identity of the building. The architect's goal was to provide a new social framework for small households, emphasizing nested scales of a community rather than individual residents.

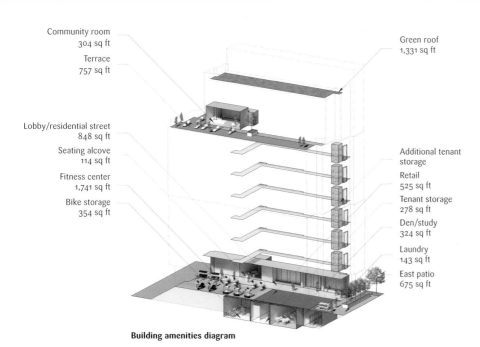

Community room
304 sq ft

Terrace
757 sq ft

Green roof
1,331 sq ft

Lobby/residential street
848 sq ft

Seating alcove
114 sq ft

Fitness center
1,741 sq ft

Bike storage
354 sq ft

Additional tenant
storage

Retail
525 sq ft

Tenant storage
278 sq ft

Den/study
324 sq ft

Laundry
143 sq ft

East patio
675 sq ft

Building amenities diagram

Communal amenities are dispersed throughout the building, encouraging residents to interact with their neighbors. Conceived as an interior street, the building's lobby is a flexible space containing lounge spaces. In the cellar, residents have access to a den, storage, bike storage, and laundry, while on the eighth floor, a community room with a pantry leads onto a public roof terrace with sweeping city views.

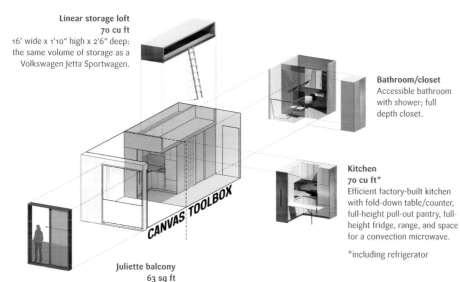

Linear storage loft
70 cu ft
16' wide x 1'10" high x 2'6" deep:
the same volume of storage as a
Volkswagen Jetta Sportwagen.

Bathroom/closet
Accessible bathroom
with shower; full
depth closet.

**Kitchen
70 cu ft***
Efficient factory-built kitchen
with fold-down table/counter,
full-height pull-out pantry, full-
height fridge, range, and space
for a convection microwave.

*including refrigerator

Juliette balcony
63 sq ft
7' wide x 9' high sliding doors and a
laminated glass guardrail.

Unit amenities diagram

The 11-foot-wide "towers" reflect the architects' intent to provide a social framework for small households by celebrating the beauty of small dimensions, while not highlighting individual micro-units on the exterior. The building's 8-foot-tall windows, placed in apartments, corridors, and stairs, recall proportions used in New York's 19th-century brownstones, one of the architects' references for the building's interior proportions.

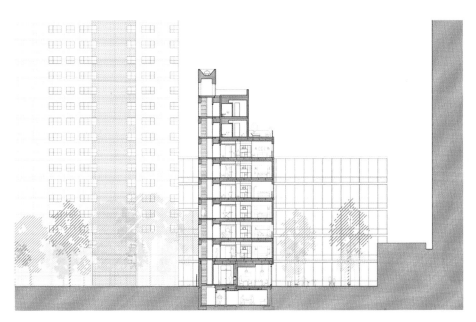

Building sections

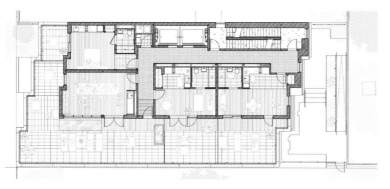

8th floor plan

The building's 5 basic micro-unit types vary in size and configuration, broadening the spectrum of choice. 40 percent (22) of the 55 rental units are designated for affordable housing, 8 of which are Section 8—reserved for formerly homeless US veterans. The remaining units (33), are market rate, half of which include furniture and services, an upgrade made possible for any of the units.

2nd–7th floor plan

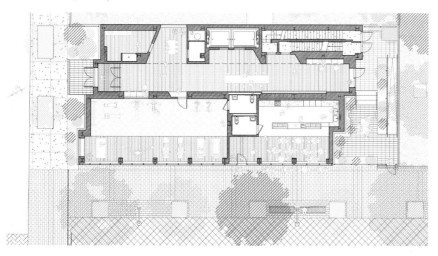

Ground floor plan

nARCHITECTS' design goals for the
unit interiors was to achieve a sense
of spaciousness and efficiency despite
their reduced area. The 9'8″ ceilings
result in a volume that is close to or
exceeds that of a regular 400-square-
foot apartment, maximizing the
perceived volume of the space.

001

Generous storage tends to be one of the top needs in every home, large or small. In small homes, well-organized storage is an additional concern. Custom cabinets are generally the best option, and while they are more expensive than their off-the-shelf counterparts, they maximize the available space, making the expense well worth it.

002

Studio apartments often rely on the multifunctional power of Murphy beds, which can transform a living room into a bedroom and vice versa in the blink of an eye.

003

Integrated cabinetry and folding furniture are space-saving solutions, optimizing functionality and creating spaces that are adaptable to different uses.

LE2 is the SoHo studio of entrepreneur Graham Hill. Like its predecessor LE1, it is the product of Graham's company, LifeEdited, a real estate development and design consultancy specializing in space optimization. But Graham Hill's design philosophy goes well beyond home design. An advocate for the environmental, financial, and emotional benefits of small-living, he aims at creating homes that positively influence people's daily lives. Learning from his first experience with LE1, he describes LE2 as "a laboratory for living with few material possessions," a tiny home where the main space is conceived as "a series of revolving scenes."

LE2 Apartment
355 sq ft

Graham Hill/LifeEdited

New York City, New York, United States

© Christopher Testani

LE2 offered the opportunity to incorporate emerging technologies like home automation devices. Insteon smart switches control all the lighting and the fan. The front door's August Smart Lock can be controlled from a smartphone.

Smart controls

Living/dining/home office configurations

Bedroom configurations

The bulk of the furniture is Resource
Furniture, including a Penelope Murphy
bed by Clei and a Passo table with
retractable legs that raise the table from
coffee to dining height. When the Penelope
bed folds into the wall, a full sofa appears.
The unit includes two recessed nightstands
with flip-down shelves.

004

Accordion doors are typically used in interiors that require flexibility in space division, more so in spaces such as conference rooms than in residential settings. They provide a level of soundproofing and insulation similar to drywall but offer the advantage that they can be folded away when not needed.

The office can be flipped into a guest bedroom, grouping seating cubes by LifeEdited to form a full or queen-size bed. This corresponds with Graham's desire to create a flexible space that is cost-conscious and durable.

005

Off-the-shelf cabinets can keep costs down and achieve the desired level of space efficiency while designing a modular kitchen around compact appliances.

006

Innovations in shower, bath, and toilet technology bring the bathroom into a new era of energy efficiency. Controls that adjust water flow and temperature are just an example. The initial investment cost might be high, but the amount of money and time saved in the long run outweighs it all.

The Pivot Apartment reimagines the studio by creating a new type of space for urban living that is flexible, sustainable, and stimulating. It is an evolution of the traditional studio apartment, where a single room accommodates sleeping, living, and dining. Inspired by a Swiss Army Knife, the apartment is a simple haven, visually unencumbered by possessions at first glance. But at any given time, the apartment can expand to reveal separate functions as needed, emphasizing openness while overlaying multifunctionality. The brief called for hosting ten for dinner, sleeping six, a home office, a private study, and an efficient kitchen for a client who loves to entertain, all within a modest 400-square-foot studio apartment.

Pivot Apartment
400 sq ft

Architecture Workshop

New York City, New York, United States

© Robert Garneau

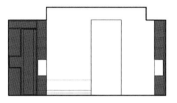

East elevation

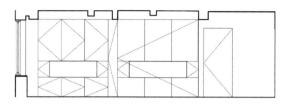

North elevation

West elevation

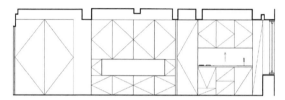

South elevation

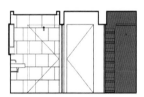

Bathroom foyer / East elevation

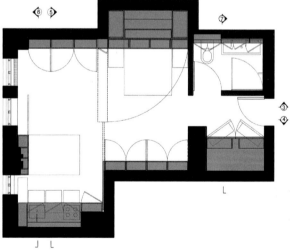

Floor plan

The kitchen features a backsplash that lifts to reveal storage behind. An expanding hydraulic table can be used for work. It can also rise at the push of a button for additional kitchen counter space.

007

Extendable tables are perfect
for tiny spaces. They maintain
the appeal for those who love to
entertain but don't have the space
to do it on a permanent basis.

The different areas are optimized for their specific uses, ranging from an enclosable bedroom, a large dining room, a separate guest sleeping area, and a private reading library.

008

A sofa bed unfolds to turn a sitting
area into a comfortable guest room,
changing the housing capacity of a
tiny home temporarily.

009

Moving partitions play their magic
on spaces, allowing for flexible
layouts that adapt to different
functions.

010

Investing in multipurpose cabinetry
is a natural progression that blurs
the distinction between architecture
and furniture, creating a seamless
combination of various functions in
small spaces.

The pivoting wall reveals a Murphy bed that supports an orthopedic mattress with a niche for power and lighting. A pair of closets on each side of the bed extend out with pulldown rods and drawers, providing generous closet space.

5:1 Apartment
390 sq ft

**Michael K Chen Architecture/
MKCA**

New York City, New York,
United States

© Alan Tansey

An outdated apartment located in a 1920s co-op building in the
Gramercy Park neighborhood of Manhattan was transformed into
a highly-functional urban micro-home, containing the practical
and spatial elements for living, working, and entertaining within
a compact area. MKCA used its expertise with transforming and
moving architecture—particularly in small residential spaces—to
create a sophisticated living environment with sensitivity to
ergonomics and the rhythms of use and space. The placement of
individual spaces and furniture favors an intelligent use of floor
space and optimizes circulation and accessibility between areas in
the transition from day to night.

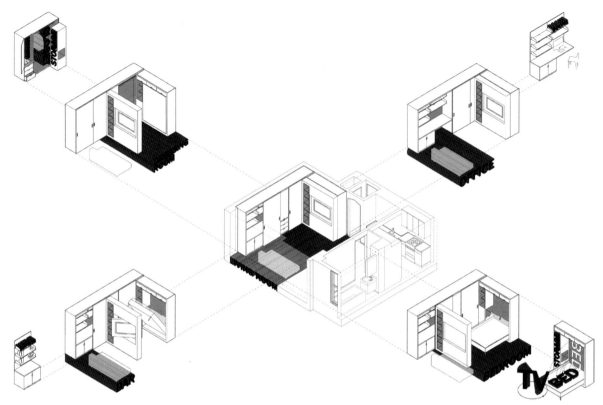

Exploded axonometric

A motorized sliding storage element glides from one end of the room to the other, creating several distinct areas within the apartment, including a living area, a home office, a kitchen, a bedroom with dressing area, and a bathroom.

011

An area of the living room can easily be used as a home office. In some cases, there might be no need to move furniture.

Various moving components and highly sophisticated hardware make possible the transformation of the space to fulfill different functions, satisfying different needs throughout the day.

012

Changing the layout of a space to accommodate different functions is a methodical process that might involve moving elements that will dramatically alter the appearance of the space, revealing parts and concealing others. Or one section of the space might take part of an adjacent section to accommodate a specific function.

013

The kitchen and the bathroom are perhaps the two spaces in a home that offer the least flexibility. This is due to the specificity of their functions, which involve plumbing and appliances.

The existing kitchen was expanded to create more working space. The new kitchen has a minimalistic design, including counters with integral sink and white lacquered cabinetry along with a generous pantry. LED lighting was installed throughout the apartment in the lighting cove above all the cabinetry, and lighting baffles were added to the underside of the existing beams.

The existing bath was thoroughly renovated and an additional linen-and-laundry hamper cabinet was added, along with a new pocket door.

Apartment in Taipei
237 sq ft

A Little Design

Taipei City, Taiwan

© Hey!Cheese

A Little Design used the renovation of an existing apartment to address coexistence issues among users of the same space. Both the architects and the client agreed that space is just as important as function when such space happens to be small. The architects turned restrictions into assets, including taking advantage of an 11-foot-high ceiling, which played a key role in the design and in the perception of the finished living space. Furnishings were arranged to ensure comfortable and functional use of the tiny space.

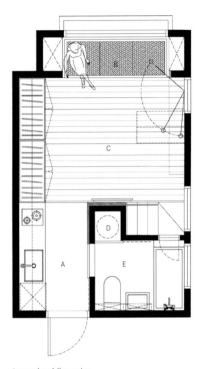

Lower level floor plan

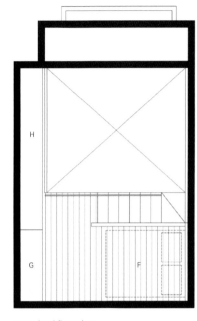

Upper level floor plan

A. Kitchen
B. Tatami
C. Living room
D. Heater
E. Bathroom
F. Bedroom
G. Desk
H. Shelf

Built-ins such as the kitchen cabinetry, closets, and bookcase line one of the walls to make the most of the high ceiling. Concentrating as much storage as possible along one area enabled the rest of the apartment to be open, allowing flexible use.

014

The tatami area under a large window makes for a bright and comfortable sitting area while also providing ample storage underneath. This sitting area pairs with the raised entry to frame the main section of the apartment in the center.

015

Multiple tables of equal proportions can come in handy to serve different purposes. High and narrow, they can lean against a wall as consoles or be joined together to form a table for eating or working.

016

The apartment's space efficiency relies on the multifunctionality of the furniture it houses. The goal was to minimize the amount of freestanding furniture in favor of built-ins such as the sitting area and the wall unit to free up as much space as possible.

017

Because the headroom on the
mezzanine cannot accommodate
a standing position, furnishing is
limited to a mattress bed and a desk.
The desk, which is an extension of
the bookcase, contributes to the
continuous flow of the space from
one area to another.

018

The apartment's minimalistic furnishing, color, and material selection—oak and white—make the space bright and spacious, compensating for the limited space area.

Despite its reduced size, the bathroom is fully fitted, with tub included. A small awning window offers enough light and ventilation, making the bathroom feel private yet airy.

Riviera Cabin

377 sq ft

LLABB

La Spezia, Italy

© Anna Positano

This project deals with the renovation of an existing apartment, which mainly involved the reconfiguration of the space to optimize functionality. The brief called for a clear separation between the living and the sleeping areas. The nautical technology—strongly bound to the Ligurian region—was fundamental to the project's detailing. The optimization of storage and the adaptation to minimal dimensions of essential functions such as cooking and bathing in sailing boats were the inspirational source of the Riviera Cabin.

Perspective sections

Floor plan

019

Organizational elements such as
the wall separating the day and
night areas can be used to integrate
functions, like storage, and conceal
plumbing lines. In addition to
organizing the space, these elements
can also serve to create pathways.

The separating wall between the day
and night areas is made of marine-grade
plywood with clear-finished surfaces
combined with white and light blue
laminated ones.

020

A combination of open and closed
storage adds to the storage
versatility of the tiny apartment,
creating opportunities for the
display of favorite items or simply
for facilitating access to items
most used.

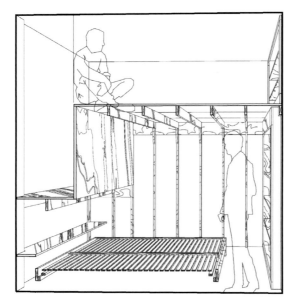

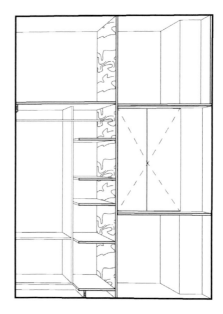

Detail section through main
bedroom and wall cabinet

The master bedroom features the
plywood wall construction, making
reference to boat building. At the far
end of the wall, opposite the front door,
a narrow staircase through a small door
leads to an attic space above the master
bedroom. With just enough room for a
bed, the tiny attic has a small opening
that looks out to the main space below.

The renovation of this compact apartment makes a bold design statement with exquisite attention to detail. A delicate approach was guided by the building's original art deco features and the designer's wish to experience the spatial possibilities the apartment had to offer. The design for the one-bedroom apartment developed by taking into account the different daily activities. Progressively, it reveals the apartment's layout through a series of inserted sculptural elements, producing stimulating sight lines, circulation paths, and separations.

Versailles
388 sq ft

Catseye Bay

Sydney, New South Wales, Australia

© Katherine Lu

The designer created the sculptural pieces of cabinetry inspired by the art deco decorative features throughout the building. Another source of inspiration was the simple integrity of artist Donald Judd's joinery created in the 1980s.

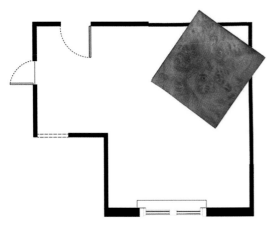

Conceptual diagram exploring the addition of a room-like joinery element to the apartment. This diagram suggests that the joinery element could produce other spaces simply through its orientation in the existing plan.

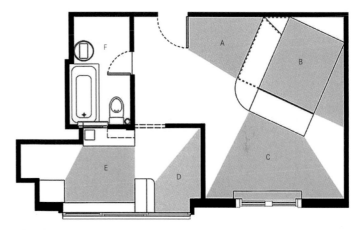

Floor plan

A. Dressing
B. Sleeping
C. Lounging
D. Eating
E. Cooking
F. Bathing

The design of this apartment is guided by two curved pieces of cabinetry fabricated in birch plywood and serving multiple functions. The location and orientation of the larger cabinet within the main space was determined by natural circulation flow and by its spatial relationship with a window, creating a cozy open space shared by the lounge and the bedroom.

The separations between different spaces aren't rigid. Rather, the different areas merge, "borrowing space" from each other, says Sarah Jamieson, director of design at Catseye Bay. Walking into the studio, the visitor is first led around a bold, sinuous, and uncompromising form—which also functions as generous wardrobe space—then swoops around to reveal the essentials required to sleep, sit, and store.

An L-shape counter-height cabinet frames the kitchen. Its shape echoes its larger counterpart, but its proportions adapt to the smaller proportions of the kitchen.

021

Materials and colors are critical design elements aimed at providing spaces with a particular feel. Their use should be restrained in small spaces, where it is easy to overdo.

Sitting on a top floor, high above a cobblestone street in the heart of Paris's sixth arrondissement, this 270-square-foot apartment serves as a pied-à-terre for a couple from the South of France. With an interior design to match its chic location, the apartment is full of character and fitted with all the basic commodities. The clients have grown fond of the "petite" proportions of their pad: "If the four walls were pushed out to 500 square feet, it wouldn't give us anything more than we have now," they say. With its beautiful light and panoramic views, this apartment is a Parisian gem.

Lovers' Pied-à-terre
270 sq ft

A+B Kasha Designs

Paris, France

© Idha Lindhag for
A+B Kasha Designs

The designers, Alon and Betsy Kasha, created a space that feels more spacious than it is by paying close attention to the proportions of the room relative to the windows, doors, cabinets, and furniture.

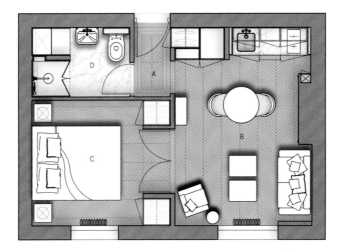

Floor plan

A. Entry
B. Living/dining/kitchen
C. Bedroom
D. Bathroom

Perspective view toward the living area and bedroom

The wall moldings and wall sconce aimed at the ceiling create the illusion of additional ceiling height. The white walls reflect the light, enhancing the feeling of amplitude, while the tan hardwood flooring adds warmth to the space.

023

The compact kitchen is opened to the dining and living area, promoting social interaction among the users of the room, making the tiny apartment perfectly suitable for entertaining a small group of guests.

What this small apartment lacks in space, it makes up for in charm and character. The all-white color scheme enhances the architectural features of the apartment and serves as a neutral backdrop for a careful selection of furniture and an art collection.

Darlinghurst Apartment
291 sq ft

Brad Swartz Architect

Darlinghurst, New South Wales,
Australia

© Katherine Lu

This tiny apartment was renovated to comfortably accommodate
a couple. The brief was simple: to design a functional apartment
suitable for living and entertaining. Generous storage spaces,
a laundry room, and a dining space were essential. However,
this seemingly modest brief understated the complexity of the
project, which was constantly bound by a small budget and tight
space constraints. While this apartment was initially one room,
the goal was to create a public and private divide to define two
distinct zones.

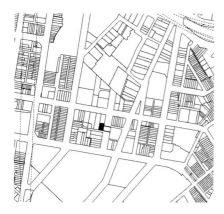

Context plan

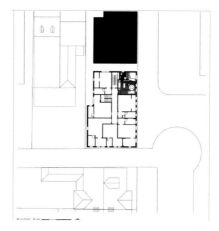

Building plan

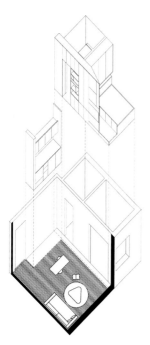

Exploded axonometric

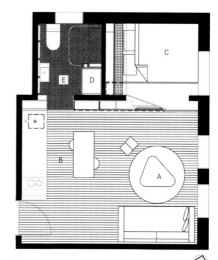

Floor plan

A. Living area
B. Kitchen/dining area
C. Bedroom
D. Laundry
E. Bathroom

A public and open living, dining, and kitchen space was formed by relocating the kitchen. A minimalist design approach was then taken to the interior design of the room to maximize a sense of space.

025

Built-ins that accommodate various
functions such as a workstation,
entertainment center, and storage
are space-saving design solutions
that allow for flexible use of a space.

The private spaces, such as the bedroom and the bathroom, required a pragmatic approach. These areas were carefully hidden behind a wall unit. Storage requirements were painstakingly considered and the bedroom was stripped back to the essential elements, mainly accommodating a bed. The storage and bed were then stacked, making the most of the limited space available.

The bed fills in the entire bedroom, leaving no underused areas.

This project was specifically designed as a short-stay accommodation and as an alternative to the shortcomings of conventional design hotels in Sydney. The existing studio apartment was compromised by poor planning with a lack of defined spaces and a comparatively oversize and underused entry. The design focuses on a contemporary plywood insertion that sits within the existing fabric of the apartment. A level change, created by the bed platform and its associated cabinetry, establishes a threshold and a visual distinction between the living and the sleeping zones while maximizing opportunities for storage and space.

Nano Pad
237 sq ft

Studio Prineas

Sydney, New South Wales, Australia

© Chris Warnes

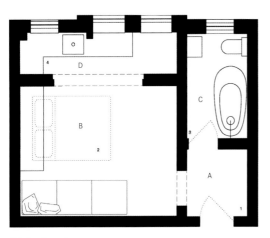

Existing floor plan

A. Entry
B. Murphy bed/living area
C. Bathroom
D. Kitchen

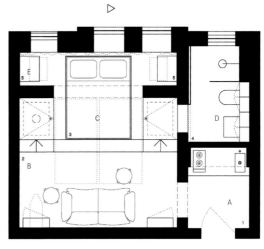

New floor plan

A. Entry/kitchen
B. Living area
C. Bed platform/underbed storage
D. Bathroom
E. Closet

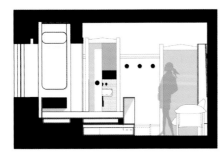

New sections

The planning of the space allows a number of functions to take place within the tiny studio apartment, providing a comfortable short-stay accommodation. Aesthetically, the inserted elements don't obscure the original art deco structure.

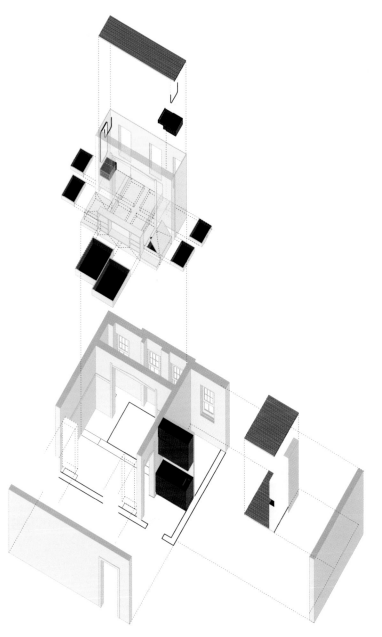

Exploded axonometric

026

The compact kitchenette contributes to the clean plan of the apartment while satisfying a guest's needs during a short-term stay.

The inserted object is made of lime-washed plywood, creating a clear distinction with the surfaces of the existing apartment. This serene environment is punctuated by black elements, including coat hooks.

Steel-framed mirrors with rounded corners are contemporary iterations of the deco features in the apartment.

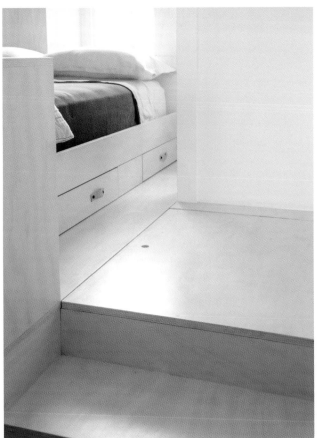

027

A level change can demarcate
different areas without having
to rely on partitions. The raised
flooring can offer the opportunity
to conceal pipes or to create
additional storage space.

This level change in the bedroom area extends into the bathroom. Raising the floor facilitated the relocation of plumbing fixtures and offered a design opportunity that resulted in a raised slatted platform that creates a sauna-like feel.

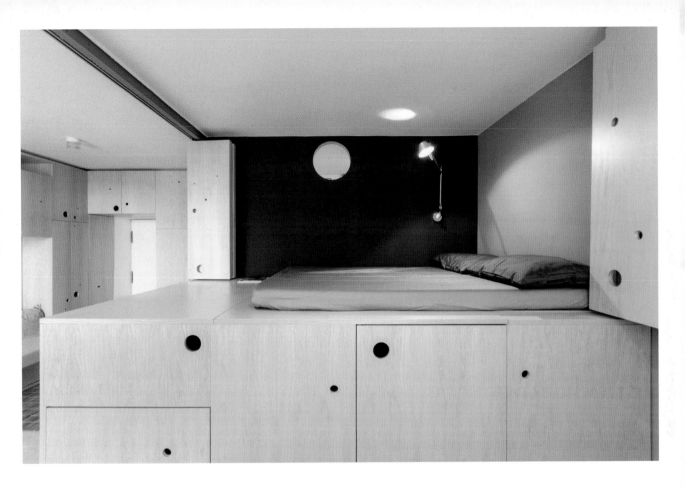

The remodel of an existing apartment was aimed at improving its plan and making the quality of its finishes consistent with its high-value location in a high-density historical building in the city center. The original conditions presented a cramped layout and a lack of natural lighting. The reorganization of the apartment was necessary, but given the space limitations, the design needed to incorporate design elements that would allow for a flexible use of the space. Flexibility was facilitated by means of rooms delimited by moving partitions, which can be closed or opened, allowing for the creation of different spatial combinations with varying degrees of privacy.

Brera Apartment
366 sq ft

PLANAIR

Milan, Italy

© Luca Broglia

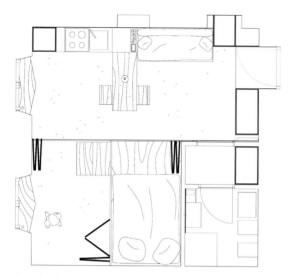

Floor plan for maximum space

Floor plan for entertaining

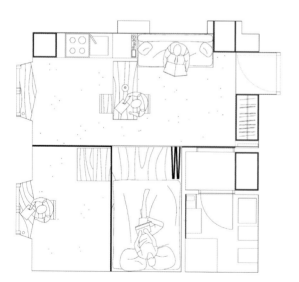

Floor plan for working

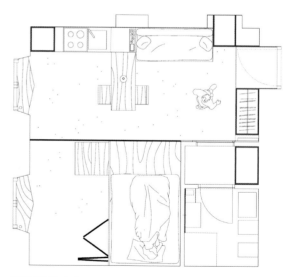

Floor plan for resting

Built-ins line the apartment's walls on three sides. These built-ins integrate all the functions of a typical living space, such as the kitchen, bathroom, and bedroom, while freeing up space for a variety of uses, like eating, entertaining, and working.

028

Projects dealing with small spaces often resort to design strategies that address technical, functional, and ergonomic issues affecting the spaces themselves and the furnishing.

A better use of the space was achieved by creating compact functional elements, freeing up floor area. This, in turn, allowed more natural light, which visually amplified the space.

029

The pieces of furniture are not just containers but are also space boundaries. They can be parts of a system that makes possible a specific function such as sleeping or a combination of functions such as working and storing.

Limited space should not be an obstacle for creative design solutions. On the contrary, it should stimulate thinking and exploring as a means to achieve the best design solution possible.

Clerestory Loft
500 sq ft

Vertebrae Architecture

Venice, California, United States

© Art Gray Photography

Built over an existing two-car garage, the project is an accessory dwelling unit (ADU) on a single-family residential lot. By definition, an ADU can be an apartment over a garage, a backyard cottage, or a basement apartment. They provide home-owners the option to house more family members or gain additional income via rent, making this a sensible move for lifestyle and financial reasons.

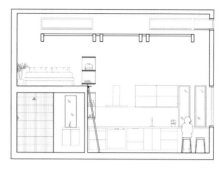

Interior elevation facing the eating and working areas

Interior elevation facing the entry

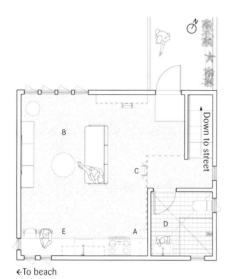

Down to street

←To beach

Floor plan

A. Eating
B. Lounging
C. Sleeping
D. Bathing
E. Working

A floating ceiling is surrounded by clerestories, providing diffused, even light in the double-height space, while the roof structure acts as an enclosure for a sunken deck above.

Two sets of stacked shelves are accessed by movable, locking ladders. While maximizing storage for the unit, they also serve as a guardrail and visual separation for the sleeping loft above.

A full kitchen provides ample counter
capacity with an adjacent area for
eating or working, concentrating three
functions into a minimal footprint.

030

Glass partitions and a curbless shower work well to expand a bathroom tight on space.

031

Loft beds are good space-saving solutions for small homes where every inch counts. They optimize tall ceiling heights and allow for program underneath.

032

Units with limited footprints
and enough height that can
accommodate two habitable levels
are fundamental to economizing
space. Going vertical affords the
space to incorporate multiple
functions such as a sleeping area,
home office, library, or storage.

Venice Micro-Apartment
330 sq ft

Vertebrae Architecture

Venice, California, United States

© Art Gray Photography

Sited 200 feet from Venice Beach, this micro-unit was commissioned by the building owner for his sole living space. The project converted an unneeded, mostly windowless laundry room into a desirable living unit. The simple yet effective design uses full-height hidden storage to delineate space and provide visual and acoustic privacy. At the same time, it addresses sustainable urban living by fitting an entire living program, including eating, sleeping, lounging, and bathing, into 330 square feet.

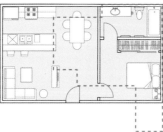

Standard Los Angeles one-bedroom
apartment: 700 sq ft

Venice Micro-Apartment: 330 sq ft

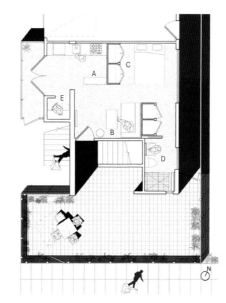

A. Eating
B. Lounging
C. Sleeping
D. Bathing
E. Working

Floor plan

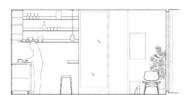

Interior elevation 1

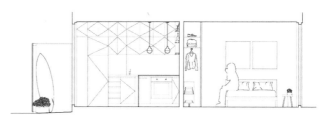

Interior elevation 2

033

The kitchen layout for tiny spaces is often limited to a straight line configuration integrating all the washing, cooking, prepping, and storing functions. This arrangement works well when the kitchen is open to the living and dining area for the most efficient use of space.

A simple material palette minimizes visual noise and maximizes the spatial quality of the apartment. Double doors to a new patio increase the amount of daylight, thus reducing dependence on energy and enhancing the perceived volume of the space. The protected balcony provides a private outdoor space that adds to the square footage of the apartment.

034

This small office shows how the generally underused space beneath a staircase can create functional space and offer opportunities for creative design solutions.

035

There is no correlation between the size of a space and its design possibilities. In other words, a large home does not necessarily have more design options than a small one.

Bazillion Apartment

484 sq ft

YCL Studio

Vilnius, Lithuania

© Leonas Garbačauskas/
AGROB BUCHTAL

YCL Studio drew a clear line between the day and the night
zones of this pied-à-terre for two. The dwelling is located
in a new residential building in the Old Town of Vilnius and
was commissioned by a frequent traveler, who uses it for
short stays. The compact apartment is essentially one open
space divided into two sections by a single ceramic-clad wall
that hints at the red bricks used throughout the Old Town
and creates two distinct moods within a very small area.
Expressing these different moods in a relatively contained
space has been the leading concept and has driven every
design decision, letting nothing divert the attention.

In this apartment, YCL's designers made one clever adaptation to conquer and divide the space: an oblique wall which splits the interior into two parts, one containing the living area and kitchen, the other the bedroom and bathroom. One is cool and open, the other is warm and concealed.

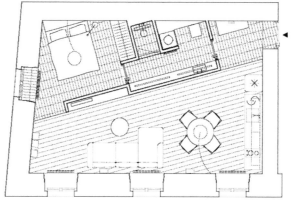

Floor plan

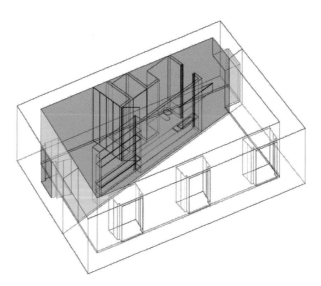

Axonometric view

036

The same color scheme can be used throughout a space, unifying various functional areas and amplifying the perception of the space.

037

The use of contrasting colors or materials maximizes the difference between parts of the same space. The colors or materials chosen can be the means to express a desired atmosphere. For instance, bright colors can be are associated with daytime zones, while dark tones are associated with nighttime zones.

The cool part has a whitewashed wooden floor, and white ceiling and walls, while the floor and walls of the warm part are clad in tiles in three shades of a terracotta color. These tiles are chosen from AGROB BUCHTAL's Goldline series. The concrete ceiling of this part of the apartment is painted in a tan color.

038

Not only is white wood versus
terra-cotta-colored ceramics
strong in itself, but it also contains
an intriguing, mysterious twist
as well. In general, light colors
make spaces look spacious and
airy. Dark colors can contribute to
the creation of cozy and secluded
rooms.

The ceramic surfaces create a warm atmosphere and, in the bathroom, easy maintenance. The design manifests the interest in liberating the ceramic tile from its common use, a use that is often limited to certain parts of the home such as the kitchen and the bathroom for practical reasons. By doing so, the design provides the apartment with an unusual and special character.

Space-Saving Interior Design
269 sq ft

Black & Milk

London, United Kingdom

© Black & Milk

A firm of London developers commissioned Olga Alexeeva to renovate a very small studio flat in the city center. This space-saving interior design task included reconfiguring the space and installing a new kitchen and new bathroom, as well as decorating and furniture sourcing. "This apartment was very petite and hadn't been touched for thirty years," says Olga. This Central London studio apartment was given new life and now works as a multifunctional space to satisfy the lifestyle of a busy professional woman who works in the media industry.

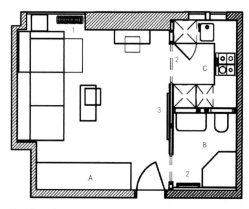

New floor plan

A. Wardrobe and study
B. Bathroom
C. Kitchen

1. Radiator
2. Pocket door
3. TV

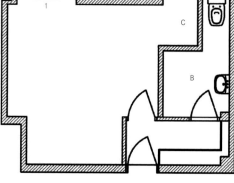

Existing floor plan

The original plan of the apartment was overly compartmentalized. The kitchen was particularly problematic, with an inefficient layout that occupied too much space. The apartment had a number of partitions which Olga removed to create a sense of space. This allowed for a large living and sleeping area with multifunctional uses.

The new plan for this small apartment satisfies the lifestyle of a busy professional woman, providing areas for working, entertaining, and relaxing.

039

The home office is concealed
behind mirrored doors, which
visually amplify the space and
reflect the light coming from the
window on the opposite wall.

040

A double bed folds down to transform the living area into a bedroom.

041

The main space is sparsely furnished to optimize flow. It can be used as a dining area to seat up to six people, a spacious sitting area to relax in or entertain, or a bedroom for resting.

The apartment incorporates a small but perfectly formed kitchen. To ensure that all the necessary appliances fitted well, Olga designed the kitchen first and then built the walls around it.

MKCA's client was seeking to turn a small and awkwardly shaped apartment on the top floor of an apartment building into a modern and multifunctional home. The project makes the most of this compact space with windows on two sides and a small attic corner. The space was aggressively yet efficiently subdivided and loaded with a custom-built transforming wall unit, which makes comfortable living, cooking, dining, working, and entertaining all possible, despite the space limitations.

Attic Transformer

225 sq ft

Michael K Chen Architecture/ MKCA

New York, New York, United States

© Alan Tansey

Floor plan for bedroom

A. Entry
B. Storage
C. Bedroom
D. Dressing area
E. Bathroom

1. Pull-out wardrobe
2. Fold-down bed
3. Wardrobe

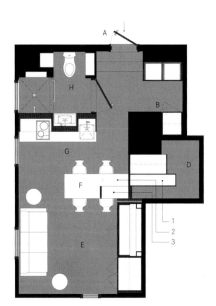

Floor plan for living room

A. Entry
B. Storage
C. Chimney
D. Attic
E. Living room
F. Dining/office
G. Kitchen
H. Bathroom

1. Pull-out pantry
2. Six-foot pull-out table
3. Pull-out computer

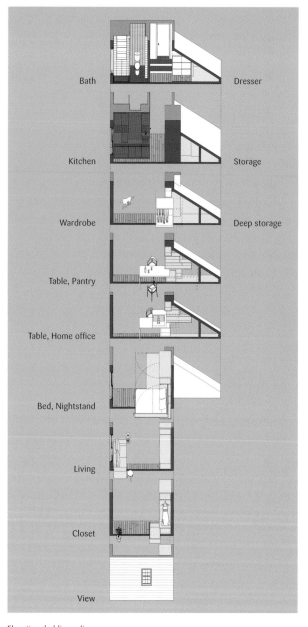

Bath	Dresser
Kitchen	Storage
Wardrobe	Deep storage
Table, Pantry	
Table, Home office	
Bed, Nightstand	
Living	
Closet	
View	

Elevational oblique diagram

Beautifully crafted custom millwork, as well as fine vintage and contemporary furnishings, make for a luxurious and youthful interior design where nothing falls out of proportion in the tiny pad.

042

Attics, like spaces beneath staircases, are difficult to use and often become underused areas that, in most cases, become cluttered up with unwanted items. However, when well planned, they can offer valuable storage space and add spatial interest to a small space.

The compact kitchen is one of the main focal points of the apartment, marking the area where cooking and eating take place. It also frames the passage between the entry area and the main room, which accommodates various changing activities.

A wall unit includes clothes storage, pantry storage, and a pull-out dining table that is paired with a pull-out workstation that converts the table into a home office with desktop computer and file cabinet.

043

Murphy beds or wall beds are
convenient space-saving features
for small rooms that allow for
flexibility without compromising
on comfort.

044

Bathrooms are perhaps one of the most challenging rooms to design in small homes, not only because of the space limitations but also because, unlike any other room in a home, they need to be enclosed, which might create a feeling of confinement.

045

The design of this small bathroom uses two design gestures to make it look inviting and spacious. It features a cool color scheme that reflects the light and floor-to-ceiling tilework that visually expands the space.

Shoe Box
172 sq ft

Elie Metni

Beirut, Lebanon

© Marwan Harmouche

Lebanese studio Elie Metni reconfigured an existing apartment for a client who rents it out on Airbnb for short-term stays. The walls and ceiling were painted white and the floor was coated in white epoxy. The entire apartment was then fitted with custom-built, space-saving furniture made of white laminate plywood. The all-white color scheme was chosen to create a bright space reflecting the generous natural lighting.

046

Furniture is arranged along the walls of the apartment to make the most of the available space, while tables and stools can be stored away when not needed so as to minimize clutter.

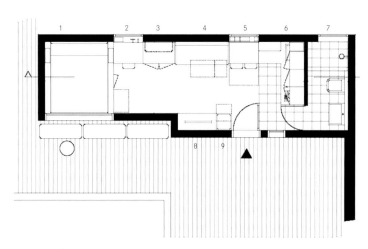

Floor plan

1. Bed
2. Desk
3. Cabinet
4. Couch
5. Dining table
6. Kitchen
7. Bathroom
8. TV unit
9. Stool

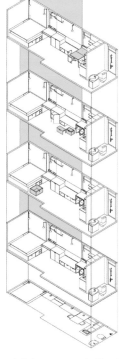

Exploded axonometric: hidden elements

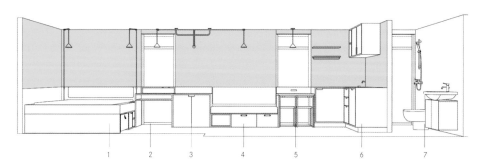

1   2   3   4   5   6   7

Perspective section

047

Storage was incorporated into almost every piece of furniture. The bed features a pull-out drawer, a cabinet, and a set of shelves. A table next to the bed can be used as a desk with an open shelf beneath and slots cut into the back to run computer and phone chargers.

Like many cities in developed countries, Beirut has become a city where finding a place to live has become a serious challenge. Space is rare and costs are high. This tiny apartment, located on the top floor of an old building in the center of Beirut, is an example of how going small is gaining popularity to stem a mounting housing crisis that affects most city dwellers. The space is small but open and brightly lit. A generously sized terrace with views of Beirut's skyline amplifies the sense of space in the tiny apartment.

Mini-Me
161 sq ft

Elie Metni

Beirut, Lebanon

© Marwan Harmouche

The brief of the client was simple and straightforward: to create a fluid space, able to accommodate up to five people and sleep two. A strong sense of space, simplicity, ease, and functionality pervades this tiny home.

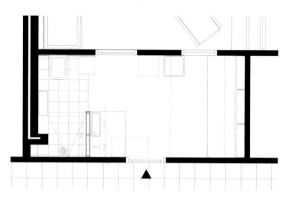

Floor plan

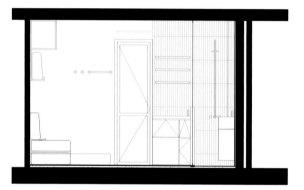

Section 1

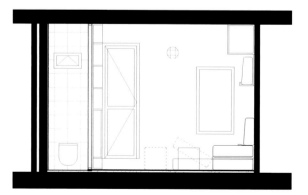

Section 2

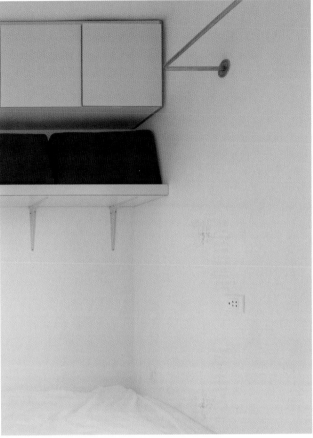

048

Storage is maximized by means of overhead cabinets and by being concealed inside various pieces of furniture such as the couch. By doing so, the designer managed to keep much of the valuable floor area free from additional furniture and accessories.

The entire unit has been designed to maximize natural lighting by creating a flexible space that can evolve and transform into efficient functions adapted for short stays.

Micropolis

Unit types 1 and 4: 200 sq ft;
Unit types 2 and 3: 300 sq ft

**Reverse Architecture and
Demeter Development Group**

Boston, Massachusetts,
United States

© Heidi Solander

Micropolis is the renovation project of a 150-year-old building with twenty very small apartments. Because of building and zoning codes, the walls between apartments remained untouched. Changes took place within each of the apartments. The initial step involved the exploration of the spatial possibilities that the building had to offer. This process evolved into the creation of four unit types. The limitations of the small units were overcome through built-ins, efficient storage, and transformable custom-made furnishings, creating flexible living spaces with a comfort level well beyond their reduced areas.

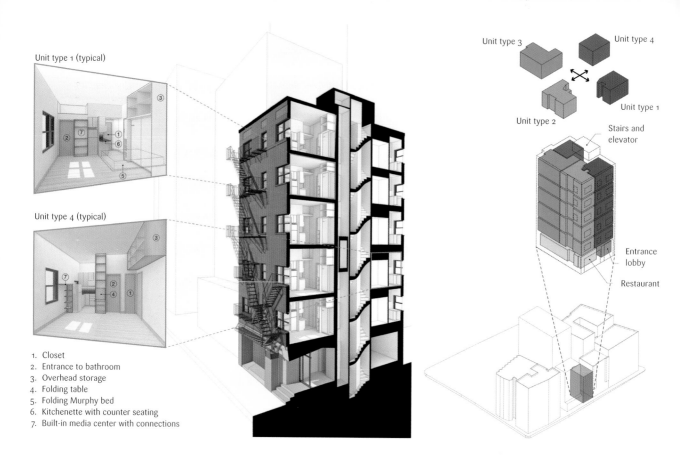

Unit type 1 (typical)

Unit type 4 (typical)

Unit type 3
Unit type 4
Unit type 2
Unit type 1

Stairs and elevator

Entrance lobby

Restaurant

1. Closet
2. Entrance to bathroom
3. Overhead storage
4. Folding table
5. Folding Murphy bed
6. Kitchenette with counter seating
7. Built-in media center with connections

In addition to upgrading the building—including the basement utilities—the design team provided the building with a new identity through the restoration of the main facade and the redesign of the lobby. The architects conducted extensive research in photo archives to unearth the history of the building.

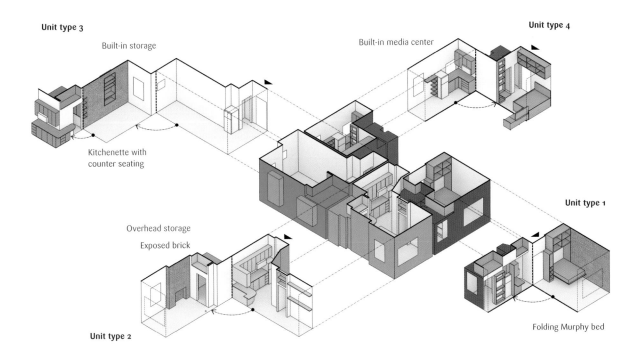

Unit type 3

Built-in storage

Kitchenette with
counter seating

Unit type 4

Built-in media center

Overhead storage

Exposed brick

Unit type 1

Unit type 2

Folding Murphy bed

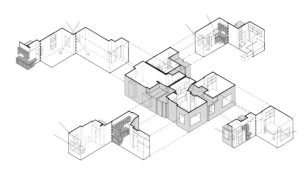

Kitchens and light

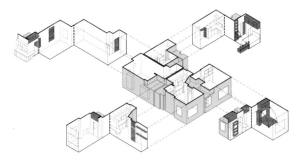

Built-in storage

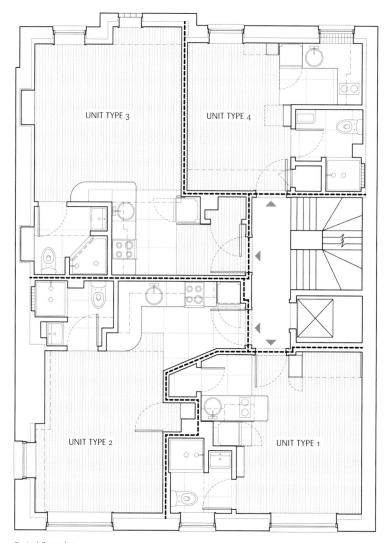

UNIT TYPE 3

UNIT TYPE 4

UNIT TYPE 2

UNIT TYPE 1

Typical floor plan

049

Murphy beds add to a room's versatility. While they might seem to be a fairly modern concept, Murphy beds—also called wall beds or pulldown beds—were introduced for the first time in the early 20th century. Their use was back then the same as it is now: basically to turn a daytime room into a bedroom or vice versa.

Removing the various layers of finishes that had accumulated over the years exposed the original and historical materials. These provided a rich backdrop for the new living spaces.

One of the larger units has ample storage, a full kitchen, comfortable zones for eating and living, and a full bathroom, all within a brightly lit open space highlighted by a restored brick chimney.

050

To make the most of the available space, the kitchen in this unit adapts to the existing floorplan, prioritizing functionality and efficiency.

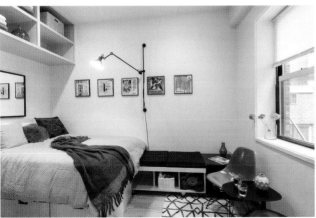

One of the smaller unit types features a compact kitchen and generous built-ins to maximize storage. The architects designed a custom trundle bed complemented with a dresser and a roll-out banquette with a coffee table and storage beneath to create a transformable space.

Compact Apartment
258 sq ft

Casa 100

São Paulo, Brazil

© Andre Mortatti

This apartment was created for an entrepreneur who splits his time between two big cities. He works in Rio during the week and spends the weekends in São Paulo. An open plan integrates a living area and a working zone. The two functions overlap, avoiding the creation of a clear demarcation between the two. This design strategy makes the most of the space, promoting an airy atmosphere that highlights the materiality of the space.

A desk creates a separation between the living and the working zone without actually creating a physical boundary that strictly demarcates these two areas. The desk can also be understood as a versatile item that can indistinctly function as an extension to the kitchen or as an entertainment center.

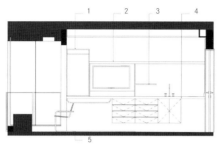

Section A1

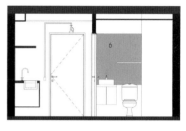

Section A3

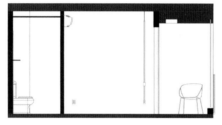

Section A2

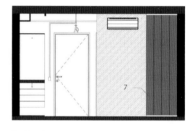

Section A4

1. Wood cabinet
2. Concrete shelf
3. MDF shelf
4. Concrete countertop
5. Wood platform
6. Mirror
7. Frosted glass

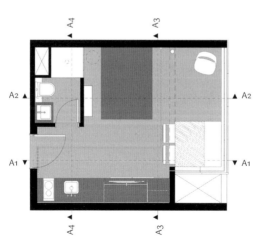

Floor plan

051

The eye-catching design of the straight-line kitchen and sliding panels made of perforated metal create a focal point. This area fulfills most of the functional needs, integrating the kitchen and storage while reserving the rest of the space for flexible use.

052

The studio opens up to a balcony large enough for a table and a pair of chairs. The apartment is small, neutral, and has multifunctional furniture that fits the owner's daily activities.

Type St. Apartment

377 sq ft

Tsai Design

Richmond, Victoria, Australia

© Tess Kelly Photography

This one-bedroom apartment can also operate as a home
office. The constraints of the existing apartment were the
lack of outdoor space and daylight, a low ceiling height,
and an inefficient kitchen. The design solution to overcome
these constraints resulted in a timber box inserted into the
apartment. The box stretches along one side of the apartment,
connecting all the spaces, and changing the perception of the
apartment from a succession of separate rooms to a series of
adjacent areas. A subdued material palette was used to bring a
sense of simplicity so as not to overwhelm the senses.

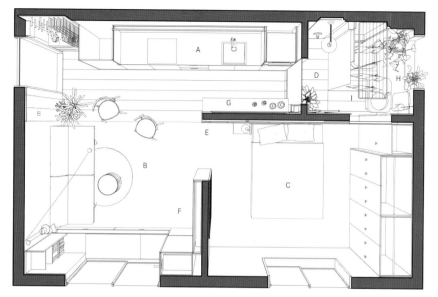

Floor plan

A. Kitchen
B. Living area
C. Bedroom
D. Bathroom
E. Dining area
   (slide out)
F. Study
G. Bar
H. Green wall
I. Drying court

N

Existing walls were, for the most part,
kept in place, as was the location
of plumbing fixtures to keep costs
down. Sliding doors contributed to the
creation of spaces that easily flow into
each other.

A clear plan and a limited material and color palette contributed to the creation of a pleasant sense of space. Natural lighting enhanced the effect. The large east-facing windows in the bedrooms and living space bathe the small apartment with abundant natural light.

053

All the wood finishes are coordinated to give a sense of uniformity and consistency, from the hardwood floor to the timber joinery box, and paneling on walls and ceiling.

054

Next to the entry, a wall unit combines a shoe rack, umbrella holder, coat hanger, and wine rack in the ultimate space-saving design solution.

The timber box is the backdrop to
the spacious living area. It contains
a 13-foot-long galley kitchen with
integrated appliances to create a clutter-
free, efficient space. The side facing
the living room has an all-black counter
with integrated sink and stove. The
opposite wall is lined with shallow open
and closed storage, marking the narrow
passage to the bathroom.

055

A compact design, paired with adequate lighting and a limited selection of materials and colors, can minimize the confined feel of a space with small dimensions.

056

A galley kitchen makes the most of
a passage between the entry and
the bathroom.

The dining table is completely hidden when not in use and the dining chairs also fold away, minimizing wasted space due to furniture. A narrow cavity between the shelves and the wall hides the dining table. It slides out via a sliding door mechanism, then folds down, creating a floating effect.

057

The sliding door between the living
area and the bedroom is made
of translucent polycarbonate,
allowing light to pass through.

One corner of the living area is dedicated to entertainment and work. The TV screen and the home office/study setup are all hidden behind cabinets, while the folding desk disappears against the wall when not in use.

Small Is Big
140 sq ft

Szymon Hanczar

Wrocław, Poland

© Jedrzej Stelmaszek

According to Szymon Hanczar, housing is primarily a shelter and, secondly, a space where one can store their personal belongings. He designed a 140-square-foot studio flat where he has lived for a year and a half. Hanczar didn't want a large apartment which, he thinks—perhaps rightly so—requires too much maintenance and care. Living large is a commodity he is willing to give up in exchange for a small pad in a city center to live the life of an urbanite. On the other hand, he was not willing to give up comfort and functionality. This conflict led him to the exploration of spatial and functional design solutions to accommodate all the essential home functions he needs within a small living space.

058

An efficient configuration of the space accommodates a small kitchenette, a bathroom, a sleeping area on the mezzanine, and even a hammock, an unexpected but welcome touch that adds casual warmth to the room.

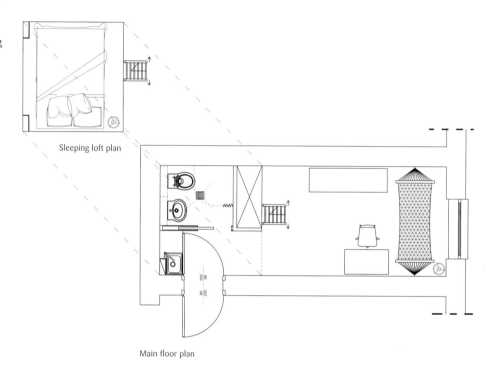

Sleeping loft plan

Main floor plan

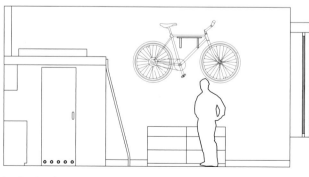

Interior elevation

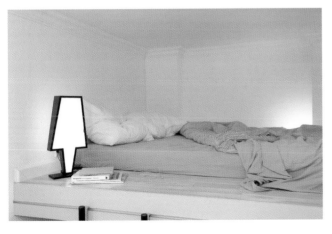

059

The only thing more fun than bunk beds is a loft bed. The elevated spot becomes a cozy area for reading and naps while offering generous usable space underneath.

060

The entire space feels bright and airy. Blond wood warms up the space, while various decorating items add color and texture. All of this contributes to the welcoming atmosphere of the space.

XS House
355 sq ft

Phoebe Sayswow Architects

Taipei, Taiwan

© Hey!Cheese

An affordable urban housing prototype envisions an organized home with fun aesthetics through a unique design language. Phoebe Sayswow Architects was invited to design a tiny guesthouse prototype for smart living in a metropolitan city. The compact apartment has an open plan organized on three levels, taking advantage of the high ceiling. This configuration offered the opportunity to create clearly demarcated areas, minimizing the need for partitions and thus maintaining the open feel throughout the entire apartment. A floor-to-ceiling wall unit lines one entire wall, offering plenty of open and closed storage. This wall unit is also a strong design feature that unifies the space and creates a sense of continuity.

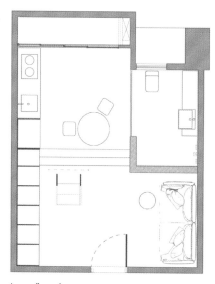

Lower floor plan

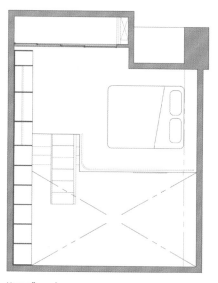

Upper floor plan

061

The design speaks a succinct and exquisite visual language through the use of materials, including birch wood and white glazed tiles with pink grout.

The potential user of the space can enjoy an inviting environment that satisfies the needs for solitary moments or for gathering times. The three levels encourage a dynamic interaction among occupants of the space.

062

The wall unit is accessible from the two levels. A movable ladder and a stair bench connect the different levels while giving a playful touch.

063

Birch wood gives a sense of
warmth, while the white glazed
tiles brighten up the space,
reflecting the light and visually
amplifying the space.

064

In small spaces, sliding doors offer interesting spatial possibilities, creating rooms that flow into each other. The use of materials that expand from one room into the next reinforces the visual continuity of adjacent spaces.

"La tournette" is the French name given to the rotating stage that is used in theaters and opera houses. This is what inspired FREAKS when they were approached by the owners of an old high-ceiling workshop with steel and architectural glass facing a quiet street in the center of Paris. They asked for a temporary living space that could evolve according to their different activities throughout the day. In response to this special request, FREAKS devised a sculptural movable bookshelf that organizes the space in various dynamic, versatile, and flexible configurations.

La Tournette

323 sq ft

FREAKS Architecture

Paris, France

© David Foessel

The old Parisian-style workshop is turned into a minimal and flexible flat accommodating all the basic living commodities while preserving the bare structure of the existing space.

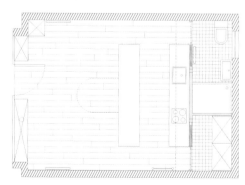

Floor plan

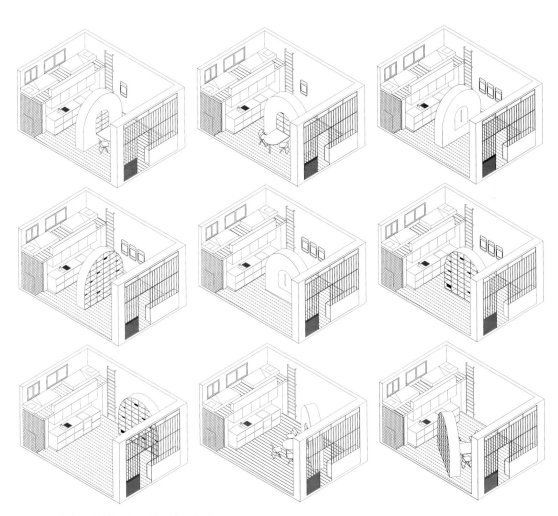

Axonometric views of different spatial configurations

065

Movable partitions promote flexibility,
allowing different uses of the space
according to different needs.

In addition to screening off the kitchen and providing shelving space, the movable wall has a folding table that, when folded down, reveals a large opening in the bookshelf that can be used as a pass-through.

The sleeping area on the mezzanine offers just enough room to sit upright when reading in bed. The kitchen's back wall extends past the mezzanine floor to contain the mattress and offer some privacy while allowing light in from the front of the space.

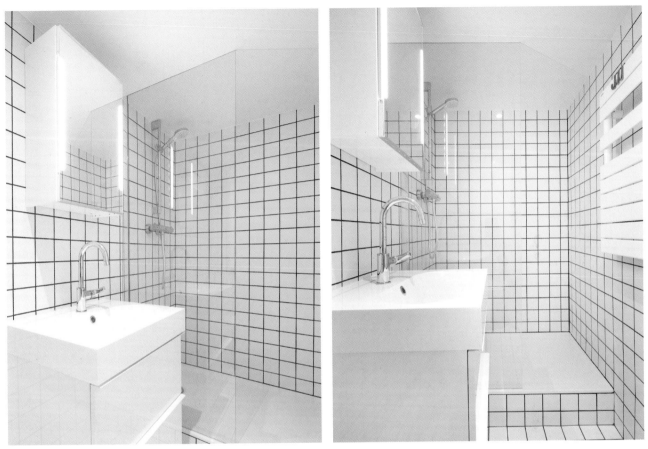

066

Challenged with the design of bathrooms—which tend to be the smallest rooms in a home—a monochromatic approach offers a clean atmosphere, avoiding visual clutter and creating a sense of simplicity and harmony.

The remodel of a city apartment never comes without challenges. Building and planning regulations, community concerns, existing conditions, space constraints, and cost, among other factors, generally influence its design expression. The creation of a dwelling within the spatial limitations of a 270-square-foot pre-existing space provides a comfortable living for a couple and their two teenage daughters without compromising comfort.

Is Space Luxury?
270 sq ft

Renato Arrigo

Sicily, Italy

© Maria Teresa Furnari

The mechanism of the bed consists
of a system of pulleys typically used
in sailboats. The system, simple and
inexpensive, requires no maintenance and
has a really low cost of implementation.

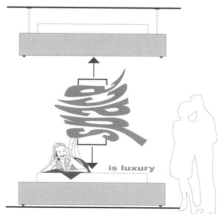

is luxury

067

In the daytime, when the bed is pulled up against the ceiling, the floor area is cleared and made available for any use.

068

The kitchen encompasses the most basic components and offers an orderly look in line with the rest of the apartment.

Floor plan

The layout of the apartment is essentially an open plan with only the bathroom as a separate room. The apartment was conceived as a single space where different activities take place. These activities are not associated with any particular section of the apartment other than the kitchen and the bathroom. Rather, the space changes throughout the day, adapting to the different activities.

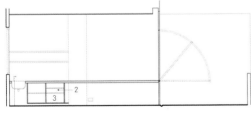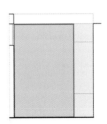

Sections

1. Oven
2. Drawer
3. Cabinet

069

The concept of a dining area is reconsidered. The dining table is replaced with a long counter along the wall as an extension of the kitchen. This is perhaps the most visible example that demonstrates the undefined limits of functional areas such as the kitchen and the dining area. Each borrows space from the other.

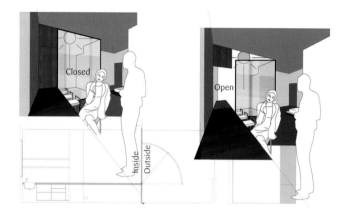

Illustrations of kitchen table and window at open and closed positions

070

The space is again transformed, eliminating the barrier between the interior space and the patio. The interior spills out onto the patio as the patio becomes part of the interior space.

This part of the apartment is furnished with movable pieces of furniture, expressing, perhaps, the temporary character of the accommodation.

While the bathroom is the only separate room of the apartment, its aesthetic is in line with the rest of the apartment's.

Montorgueil Apartment

280 sq ft

Atelier Daaa

Paris, France

© Bertrand Fomperyne

This tiny studio's plan is organized along two axes that define a modular layout and changes in materials and finishes, all with minimal partitioning. This design contributes to the creation of clearly demarcated areas that emanate functionality while maximizing an open feel. A central cabinet, integrating numerous daily-life home components, is key to changing the function of the main space. At the same time, the changes in use of the space bring with them a transformation of the apartment's atmosphere.

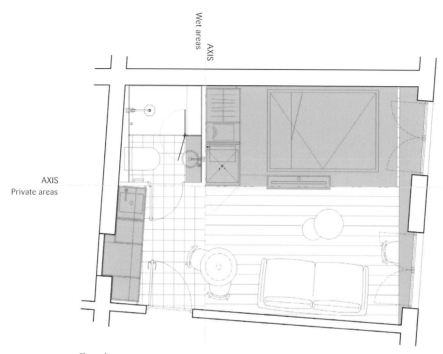

Wet areas

AXIS

AXIS
Private areas

Floor plan

071

A change of materials can
demarcate different areas. This
design element avoids the need
for the creation of partitions and
favors openness.

072

A straight-line kitchen is space efficient and works well with open spaces promoting fluid circulation.

The wall unit integrates storage. It plays
a critical role in the creation of different
settings, exposing some parts of the
apartment while concealing others.

The plinth under the bed offers very valuable storage space, while a deep window sill at the foot of the bed can be used as a desk.

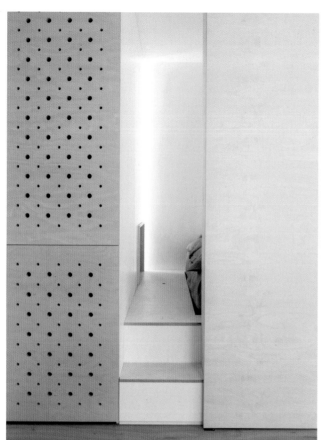

073

The sliding panel alters the space, creating different sight lines and exposing hidden areas. Sliding doors have a transformative power that swing doors don't have.

Boneca Apartment
258 sq ft

Brad Swartz Architects

Rushcutters Bay,
New South Wales,
Australia

© Tom Ferguson

Aptly named Boneca Apartment—*doll's house* in Portuguese—by the client, this apartment has a sense of luxury and refinement way beyond its size. The design team approached the remodel of this apartment utilizing two complementary design tactics to create a discrete separation between the public and the private spaces. A floor-to-ceiling sliding hardwood screen is the key device for expressing this separation. More than half of the apartment's area is free from any partition to make room for an open living and dining area. The kitchen, bedroom, bathroom, wardrobe, and storage were then arranged behind the screen, all interlocking like *Tetris* pieces.

The apartment receives abundant natural light through a long band of windows facing south.

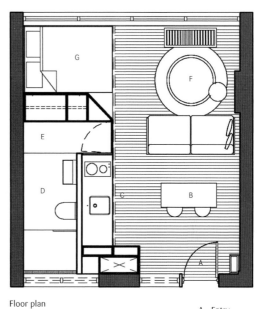

Floor plan

A. Entry
B. Dining area
C. Kitchen
D. Bathroom
E. Wardrobe
F. Living area
G. Bedroom

1. The location of the timber screen defines the function of the apartment at any time.

2. All functions of the apartment—kitchen, bathroom, wardrobe—are fitted together like *Tetris* pieces.

3. A tightly packed core creates a living space comparable to that of a small one-bedroom apartment.

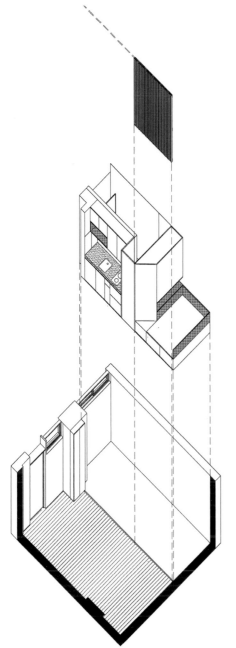

Exploded axonometric

The entry door is opposite the long band of windows. This influences the perception of the space, which appears bright and open.

The hardwood screen runs perpendicular
to the windows and guides the circulation
from the entry door into the heart of the
apartment without affecting the visual
sense of the space and allowing natural
light and airflow.

Assisting the screen is the bedroom's angled wall that broadens the sight line on entering the apartment, to take in the full width of the windows. The bedroom is reduced to bare essentials, accommodating a double bed with bulk storage below and a recessed shelf beside.

074

The bathroom and dressing area flow
into each other for a seamless effect
and most efficient use of the space.

075

The ceiling in the bathroom seems to float above a transom window. Cove lighting washes the tiled wall and enhances the floating effect of the ceiling.

Atelier_142
484 sqft

Atelier Wilda

Paris, France

© David Foessel

This project consists of the renovation of French painter Pierre Lemaire's old studio to create a minimalist loft in the heart of Paris. The existing interior was gutted, maintaining only the load-bearing walls and the roof. The resulting blank slate offered the possibility of organizing the space and creating new partitions according to the client's needs and lifestyle. From the beginning, one aspect of the new design both the architect and the client agreed upon was to maintain the open character of the space as much as possible, maximizing the use of built-in furniture.

The small house is accessed through a gate on a quiet cobblestone street. The gate leads to a private paved courtyard where the single-story building stands, enjoying privacy and some open space at the doorstep to make up for the reduced interior area.

076

Skylights offer additional natural lighting. Light coming from different sources, such as from skylights and windows, provides spaces with even lighting, minimizing harsh light and shadow contrasts.

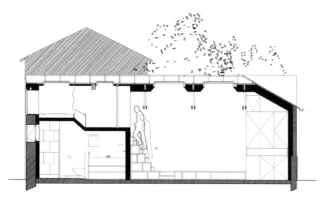

Longitudinal section

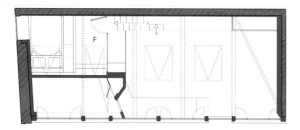

Upper level floor plan

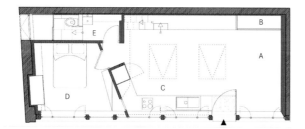

Lower level floor plan

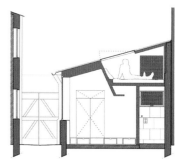

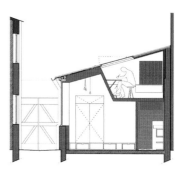

Cross sections

A. Living area
B. Closet
C. Kitchen
D. Bedroom
E. Bathroom
F. Loft bed and
   home office

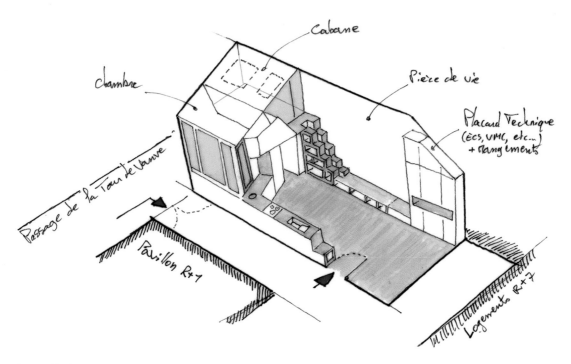

Cabane

Chambre

Pièce de vie

Placard Technique
(ÉCS, VMC, etc...)
+ rangements

Passage de la Tour de Vanve

Pavillon R+1

Logements R+7

Axonometric view

Maintaining the architectural quality of the original space was a crucial design goal. This was achieved by using minimal partitioning and by arranging all the functional components and furniture along the perimeter walls to free as much floor area as possible.

The stepped design of the cabinetry seems to be inspired by the Japanese *tansu* step chest. It highlights the horizontality of the loft and guides the circulation from one end of the space to the other.

077

Limited color and material enhances the sense of space. The white surfaces, including walls, ceiling, and cabinetry highlight the wood details while softening and warming up the space.

A simple bathroom layout makes the most of the small area. With no tall elements interfering with the continuity of the space and a frosted glass awning window providing plenty of natural light and ventilation, the bathroom is a private and inviting corner of the house despite its reduced dimensions.

078

All the furniture has been customized and designed down to the smallest detail in order to maximize storage capacity and clear up as much space as possible.

The client asked that the new home have a guest room despite the limited space available. Confronted with this challenge, the architect proposed a sunny "cabin" perched above the main floor that integrates a double bed and a workspace with storage and a foldaway desk.

Tiny Hideaways

FREAKS was commissioned for the refurbishment of a preexisting concrete fishing shack of ten by fifteen feet, built in the rock during the 1950s. Because of the strict coastal construction regulations, the shack couldn't change in size or shape. The architects realized that the shack's dimensions and ratio were comparable to those of the log cabin on Walden Pond, where philosopher Henry David Thoreau lived alone for two-and-a-half years. During this time, Thoreau focused on nature, his writing, and "to front only the essential facts of life," he wrote. This concept, so profusely revived nowadays through many small house trends, was the starting point for the project, manifesting that downsizing isn't necessarily a sacrifice.

Viking Seaside Summer House
129 sq ft

FREAKS Architecture

Fermanville, France

© Jules Couartou

The minimalistic interior consists of a white-tile and yellow-grout core containing the bathroom and a loft bed that sleeps two people. The compact kitchen is open to the main living area, while a large terrace expands the living space to the stunning seaside pink granite landscape.

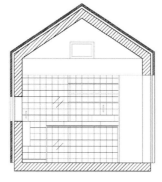

North interior elevation

South interior elevation

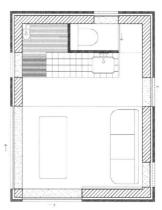

Ground floor plan

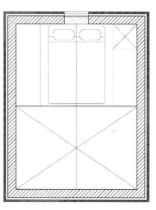

Mezzanine floor plan

079

The lounge area is equipped with a couch and a table that seats eight people.

080

The pitched roof is a representation of the stereotypical form for shelter.

Tucked away in a clearing surrounded by ninety-nine acres of forest, this finely crafted cabin provides shelter for some time off the grid in both a literal and metaphorical sense, exploring the essence of retreat and re-connection to nature. The owner's desire to build small and a childhood spent in traditional Japanese houses set the guidelines for the design of a cabin that reconciles the owner's love of Bruny Island, her culture, and her minimalist ideals.

Bruny Island Hideaway
301 sq ft

Maguire + Devine Architects

Bruny Island, Tasmania, Australia

© Rob Maver

Turning away from tall trees and a dark
forest to the north, the cabin addresses
long views to the south from a daybed
and opens up to east and west decks.

081

The space restrictions of small areas become unimportant when there is a chance to expand the interior to the exterior and enjoy open-air living to its fullest.

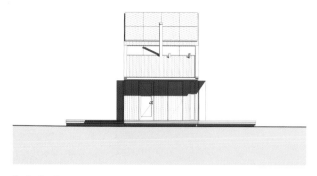

North elevation

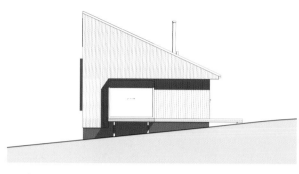

East elevation

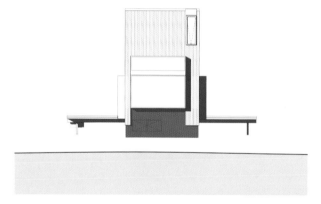

South elevation

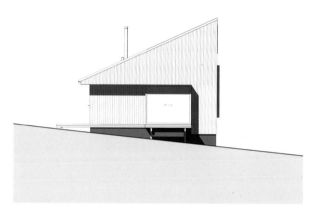

West elevation

A high roof elevates solar panels and
a skylight to catch the sun from over
the trees, while the metal-clad exterior
keeps the rugged coastal weather out.

082

The mezzanine floor adds usable square footage to the small cabin. Living small doesn't necessarily mean that there is no room for comfort.

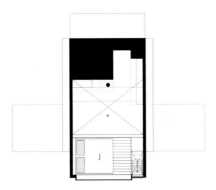

Mezzanine floor plan

Main floor plan

A. Living
B. Daybed
C. Bathroom
D. Entry
E. Study
F. Laundry
G. Kitchen
H. Morning deck
I. Afternoon deck
J. Sleeping loft

N

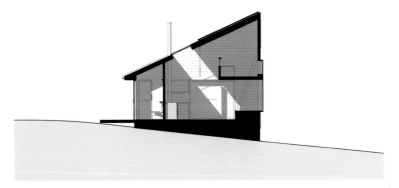

Section

The multileveled interior creates an
interesting spatial experience further
enhanced by the generous openings that
offer framed views of the surrounding
landscape. The cabin experience is not
limited by the wall boundaries but it is
expanded to the outside. A dialogue
is established between interior and
exterior, thus satisfying the desire to
reconnect with nature.

In contrast with the rough skin of the
cabin, the interior is made of light-
colored timber that creates a warm,
cozy sense of enclosure, referencing
not only Japanese architecture but also
remote wilderness cabins from all over
the world, evoking a sense of distance
and escape.

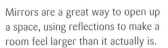

083

Mirrors are a great way to open up a space, using reflections to make a room feel larger than it actually is.

Knapphullet

323 sq ft

Lund Hagem

Sandefjord, Norway

© Ivar Kvaal, Kim Muller,
Luke Hayes

Knapphullet is a small annex to an existing holiday home with the Norwegian coastal landscape as a stunning backdrop. Accessible only by boat or by foot through a dense forest, the small hideaway is wedged between large outcrops and surrounded by low vegetation for wind protection. The design developed from the desire to echo the roughness and beauty of the surrounding landscape. This led to the distinct shape of the building: a stepped ramp with a lookout roof encasing a compact shelter. This hideaway encompasses adequate orientation to make the most of natural lighting and a compact open plan that spills out onto a series of outdoor areas conceived as gathering spaces to enjoy good weather.

084

The building adapts to the
surroundings with the principles
of scale.

While the roof terrace offers a panoramic view of the stunning scenery, the view from the house is more restricted. Instead, the views from inside the house focus on the more intimate aspects of the surrounding landscape: the texture of the rock surface, and seasonal changes in the vegetation.

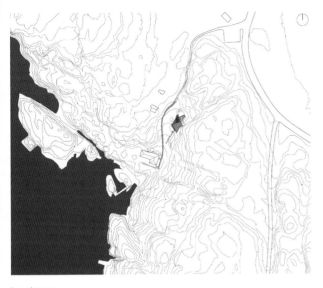

Location map

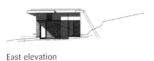

East elevation

South elevation

West elevation

North elevation

Although the building occupies a small footprint, the space expands vertically over four levels, including a roof terrace. Accessible via a long boarded walkway, the house offers a sheltered atrium formed by the building and the outcrops.

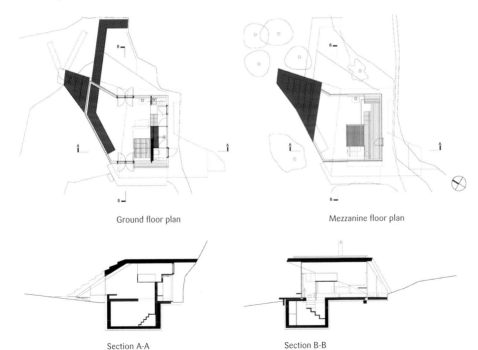

Ground floor plan

Mezzanine floor plan

Section A-A

Section B-B

The east-facing atrium receives the morning sun, while the west-facing terrace opens toward the evening sun. The use of skylights takes further advantage of the long daylight hours experienced during the summer. There is a roof opening right against a rock, allowing daylight to pour down into the entrance and the bathroom.

085

A long concrete bench and flooring extend from the interior to the exterior, exemplifying a design strategy aimed at minimizing the indoor-outdoor separation.

Despite its reduced dimensions, Knapphullet contains an open living area with a small bathroom and a loft bed that sleeps two people. Thanks to the generous spans of glass the interior doesn't feel confined but rather airy, taking in the views of the Nordic coastal landscape.

The "Carpineto Mountain Refuge" was an architectural competition for students and young architects organized in 2015 by Archistart (www.archistart.net). The competition was aimed at promoting the touristic appeal of the Lepine Mountains in central Italy. One of the main design goals was to express the cultural and geographical character of the region through a series of temporary refuges to be located along the main hiking paths. The winner of the competition is the project designed by Gnocchi+Danesi Architects, who described their design as a contemporary interpretation of old traditional mountain refuges, bringing in architectural character and spatial quality.

Carpineto Mountain Refuge
215 sq ft

Gnocchi+Danesi Architects

Rome, Italy

© Gnocchi+Danesi Architects

The refuge is designed with sustainability in mind, both in the choice of materials and in the use of passive and active energy systems. It evokes an archetypal form using contemporary construction principles.

20mq

1   2   3   4   5

Structure

A prefabricated wood construction system was devised to facilitate the construction on a site with difficult access.

Expandability

Each module has an independent structure, allowing freedom of configuration and expansion.

Water

The refuge is fitted with a rainwater collection system.

Exterior cladding

One of the modules has a roof with photovoltaic panels.

Concept

Floor plan and elevations

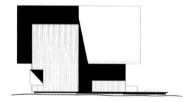

Relax   Dinner for six   After dinner

Layout options

Different layout configurations offer the possibility to manage space according to the needs.

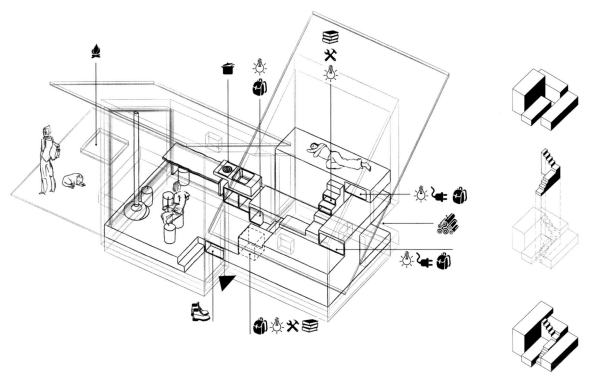

Spatial diagram

086

To each his own space. The interior design makes the most of the limited area, creating a comfortable space.

087

The rustic appeal of the mountain refuge provides a unique atmosphere that stimulates and expands a vacation experience.

088

This refuge provides comfortable accommodation full of old-world charm and a warm and friendly atmosphere.

Taylored Architecture was asked to design a "tiny house" or "love shack" for a client as a surprise gift for her and her husband's twentieth wedding anniversary. The client desired a contemporary aesthetic with efficient spaces. Different materials, textures, and patterns combine with clear-finished plywood panels that unify the whole interior.

Thurso Bay Love Shack
328 sq ft

Taylored Architecture

Grindstone Island, New York, United States

© Eric Salsbery

A standing seam roof wraps down the back exterior wall of the structure, while large windows and doors facing the Saint Lawrence River bring the outside in.

089

The setting of a house and its orientation is key to determining the placement and sizes of windows to optimize natural lighting, ventilation, and views. Windows not only influence an interior design but also how space is perceived by its occupants.

Northeast view

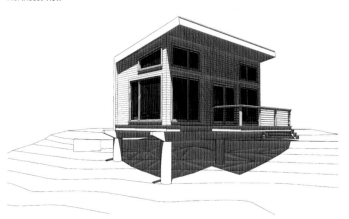

Southeast view

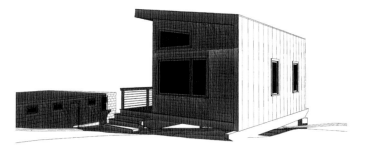

Northwest view

North elevation

East elevation

South elevation

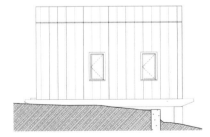

West elevation

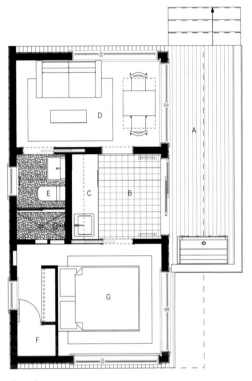

Floor plan

A. Deck
B. Entry
C. Kichenette
D. Living/dining area
E. Bathroom
F. Utility
G. Bedroom

The main room of the Love Shack has big windows that let abundant natural light in and visually open up the interior to the exterior. The brightly lit space looks comfortable and warm, thanks to the hardwood flooring and plywood paneling on the walls and ceiling. Sparsely furnished, the room affords an accent wall featuring a Mondrian-like composition made of different color-stained wood panels.

Vivid colors, textures, and patterns animate the cabin, providing each area of the cabin with its own identity while creating flow among them.

090

Pops of color and texture must be used carefully in small spaces, as using them in excess can be overwhelming. They can be mixed with neutral colors or materials throughout to visually connect contiguous spaces and to create a harmonious balance.

The bathroom is another display of color, texture, and pattern. A dark-colored running bond tile pattern on the walls, a river rock floor, and a plywood ceiling coexist beautifully despite the reduced area. The combination creates a clean yet warm atmosphere.

The Oak Cabin combines refined Scandinavian design with traditional craftsmanship, creating an environment that enables its occupants to re-engage with the simple pleasures of cabin life. It was conceived as a sustainable low-impact dwelling that is equally suited to use in the countryside or at the end of an urban garden. McKelvie was trained as a wooden-boat builder and worked in the furniture industry before establishing Out of the Valley in 2015 at his farm. "I have always had an interest in small-scale architecture, and after I built my first cabin it was clear that there was a demand for my craft," said McKelvie.

Oak Cabin
259 sq ft

**Rupert McKelvie/
Out of the Valley**

Devon, United Kingdom

© Rupert McKelvie

The burnt wood gives a dark finish that enables the building to blend in with the shadows of a wooded setting. In contrast, the interior features a whitewashed ash kitchen, furniture, and paneling.

259 sq ft
(+mezzanine 71 sq ft)

22 x 12 ft
h = 14 ft

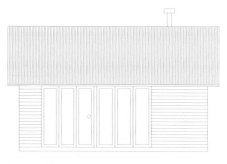

Front elevation

Section

Floor plan

Building-frame axonomentric view

Wood for the cabins is sourced from
sawmills local to the site and prepared
by McKelvie and his team to make it
ready for construction. The designer is
also always on the lookout for storm-
fallen trees that can be cut into planks,
dried, and used later for indoor furniture.

091

The cabin combines traditional timber-frame construction methods with modern details. The Oak Cabin has a traditional trussed framework that can be erected in just two days.

092

A wood-burning stove provides
heating, with photovoltaic panels
on the roof generating electricity to
help power lighting and a convection
oven. The cabin can be connected to
a water supply to provide water to
the kitchen and bathroom.

093

The cabin features a whitewashed ash kitchen, furniture, and wall paneling, as well as oak flooring, and natural linseed-painted bifold doors and windows.

Inverness Bathhouse

260 sq ft

Richardson Architects

Point Reyes, California,
United States

© Jeff Zaruba

This small building was designed to accommodate a large group
of children for a yearly family summer camp. It is sited among
a cluster of farm buildings and is designed to blend with the
environment of the pastoral dairy farm. The property provides
welcoming and comfortable amenities for the nearby tent
platforms and sleeping quarters. The design concept embraces
a fun, whimsical, and practical character that evokes the rural
quality of the property.

094

A porch wraps around two sides of the building, creating a sheltered outdoor space where the interior can spill out. Porches and terraces are a luxury that takes small living to another level.

Side elevation

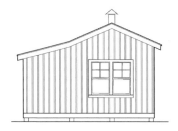

Back elevation

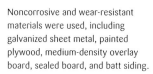

Noncorrosive and wear-resistant materials were used, including galvanized sheet metal, painted plywood, medium-density overlay board, sealed board, and batt siding.

Side elevation

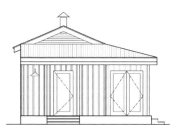

Front elevation

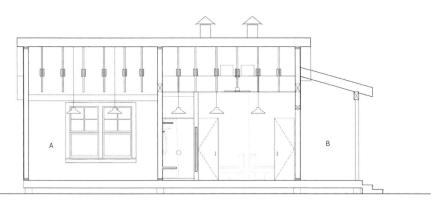

Section

A. Bedroom
B. Porch

095

The barn aesthetic makes for a casual living experience: built-ins, efficient basic kitchen, plenty of light, and vistas.

PV Cabin is used as a temporary shelter for a young couple of rock climbers. The location stands out for its mountainous landscape that hosts a wide variety of adventure sports. Located in a small clearing surrounded by a densely wooded area at the foot of a high cliff, the site is accessed via a winding road. This open space in the middle of the forest ensures breezes and natural light. The cabin stands on wooden piles five feet above the ground to avoid contact with snow during the winter season. The main challenge of the design was the limited footprint, but the physical ability of the users allowed the designer to increase the surface vertically.

PV Cabin
258 sq ft

Lorena Troncoso-Valencia

Pinto, Chile

© Cristóbal Caro

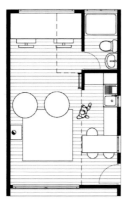

Lower floor plan

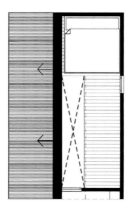

Mezzanine floor plan

Roof plan

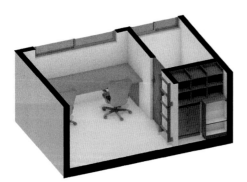

Perspective section

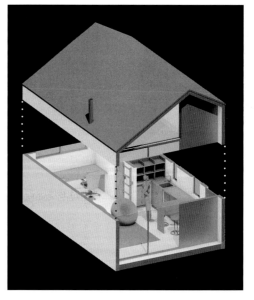

Exploded axonometric

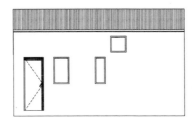

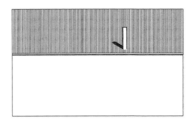

Elevations

Sections

The natural setting inspired the cabin's form and materiality. This led to the asymmetrical shape of the cabin, which echoes the verticality of the mountain behind it. At the same time, this feature has functional purposes. The pronounced slope of the roof allows for adequate runoff and creates a generous sense of amplitude and a cozy atmosphere in the interior.

The asymmetrical shape of the roof strengthens the plan of the cabin, making a clear distinction between a full-height living area behind the glass and a two-level configuration of spaces behind the wood section, including a bathroom, kitchen, dining area, and loft bed with storage space above.

The cabin's exterior and interior are finished in the same wood so as to emphasize its materiality and form. Wood also gives the cabin a natural character that is reminiscent of the traditional log construction.

096

There is room for basic living activities during short periods of time, including minimal space for sleeping, eating, washing, and allowing extra space for itinerant guests.

097

The pitched roof above the loft
bed provides a sheltering feeling
similar to a warm hug.

Redsand Cabins

300 sq ft (each)
(two cabins combined)

**Colorado Building Workshop at
CU Denver + DesignBuildBLUFF
at the University of Utah**

In the desert near Monument
Valley, Colorado, United States

© Jesse Kuroiwa

The Mexican Water Chapter of the Navajo Nation partnered with
the University of Colorado Denver and the DesignBuildBLUFF
program to design and build two rentable cabins to bolster
the local tourism industry. Influenced by the landscape and
distant views of the Blue Mountains and Monument Valley, the
programmatic design and materiality led to the development
of two "sibling" cubes, named Sunrise and Sunset. In order to
diversify the sleeping arrangement possibilities between the two
300-square-foot spaces, the Sunrise Cabin includes a two-person
sunken bed platform, and the Sunset Cabin, with a bed, loft, and
futon, can sleep up to six visitors.

The orientations of the Sunrise and Sunset Cabins were influenced by the Navajo tradition of eastern entry. While entering the Sunset Cabin requires a journey through the patio first, the journey of the Sunrise Cabin is through the building and out toward the cantilevered patio.

One cabin rests on the landscape while the other emerges from it. Each cabin establishes its own identity while together simultaneously evoking the same language.

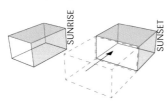

Fig. 1 Shift the volumes to mazimize views
and allow privacy

SUNRISE SUNSET

Fig. 2 Box within a box delineates space
in living area

SUNRISE SUNSET

Fig. 3 Sunrise Cabin is a journey outward;
Sunset Cabin is a journey inward

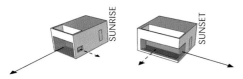

SUNRISE SUNSET

Fig. 4 Patio spaces maximize primary and secondary
views to Monument Valley and Blue Mountain

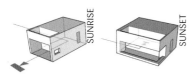

SUNRISE SUNSET

Fig. 5 Solar axes align apertures with equinoxes
and connect the cabins to the earth

SUNRISE SUNSET

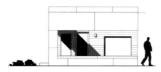

Sunrise Cabin's north elevation

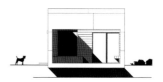

Sunset Cabin's north elevation

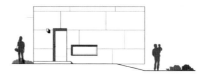

Sunrise Cabin's east elevation

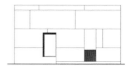

Sunset Cabin's east elevation

Sunrise Cabin section

Sunset Cabin section

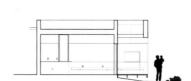

Sunrise Cabin's floor plan

A. Entry
B. Bathroom
C. Kitchen
D. Living area
E. Bed platform
F. Patio

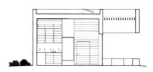

Sunset Cabin's floor plan

A. Entry   G. Egress
B. Patio   H. Bathoom
C. Fire pit   I. Bedroom
D. Dining area J. Closet
E. Living area K. Lofted bunk
F. Kitchen

098

Both patios, located on the northern side of the cabins, provide shade in the summer and are clad in reclaimed barn wood.

099

Beauty and craft can be seen
in the treatment of interior and
exterior finishes. Concrete floors,
sinks, and counters contrast with
the reclaimed barn wood on the
interior walls, while the weathered
steel exterior echoes the red sand
of the landscape.

100

Openings in both cabins frame views of the surrounding natural environment: the sand, the mountains, and the sky. Natural light through windows and the skylight complements electrical lighting to fill the spaces with a soft glow to highlight materiality.

In 2016, the Colorado Outward Bound School (COBS), a not-for-profit organization focusing on outdoor education, and the University of Colorado Denver's Colorado Building Workshop continued their partnership to create a second project. A group of twenty-eight students designed and built seven insulated cabins for year-round use. The cabins featured the same village housing boundaries as the fourteen seasonal cabins constructed two years earlier: deep within a lodgepole pine forest and accessible only by a narrow dirt road. The small cabin footprints, LED lighting, and the high-insulation properties of the structural insulated panels (SIPs) combined with the snow's natural insulation to create highly energy efficient living environments.

COBS Micro-Cabins
100 and 200 sq ft

Colorado Building Workshop at CU Denver

Camp near Leadville, Colorado, United States

© Jesse Kuroiwa

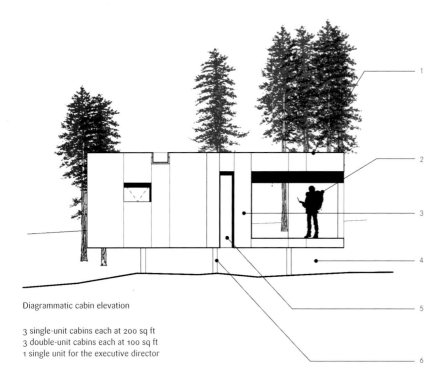

1. Flat roof holds snow in the winter for an additional R-30 insulation.
2. Private "compressed" decks for introverted senior outward bound guides.
3. Hot-rolled steel cladding used as a rainscreen to protect the cabin.
4. Under cabin storage for large items, including kayaks, skis, bikes, etc.
5. Custom 3MVI-B taped glazing at all fixed windows.
6. Steel subframe using moment connections to support structurally insulated panel frame. It utilizes the structure that already exists in the SIP to carry the load.

Diagrammatic cabin elevation

3 single-unit cabins each at 200 sq ft
3 double-unit cabins each at 100 sq ft
1 single unit for the executive director

Students were required to conduct a critical architectural inquiry into materiality, structure, light, context, environment, and program to create innovative solutions to prefabricated accelerated-build micro-housing.

Each 200-square-foot cabin was required to house one or two residents and be powered by a single electrical circuit. The circuit provides lighting, heating, and a series of receptacles with the capacity to charge technology and small appliances (mini refrigerators, teakettles, coffee pots, etc.). A central staff lodge is accessible to the residences for bathing, cooking, and laundry.

The orientation and articulation of each of the seven cabins react individually to the immediate site conditions present in the landscape. The cladding and the vertical columns of the moment frame below blend with the pine forest, minimizing the visual impact. Hot rolled steel cladding provides a low maintenance rain screen for the structure.

101

The students adapted the logic of "snow insulation" for their structures, inspired by *quizees*, a snow shelter made from a hollowed-out pile of snow.

102

No two cabins are alike, offering
diversity. The different floor plan
types respond to the need for
different types of accommodations.

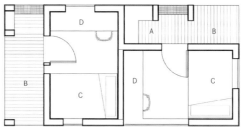

Cabin A floor plan

A. Outdoor mudroom
B. Deck
C. Bed with storage
D. Desk and built-ins

While all seven cabins are different in configuration, they are all finished in the same materials; hot rolled-steel cladding outside and birch plywood inside, bringing warmth to the structure and evoking a connection with the trees surrounding the site.

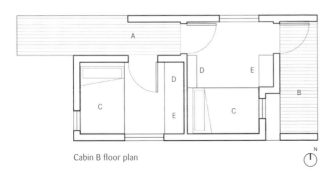

Cabin B floor plan

A. Entry walkway
B. Deck
C. Bed with storage
D. Built-ins
E. Desk

Cedar-clad front and back porches are carved from the main mass to create entries and private outdoor spaces for the more introverted permanent COBS staff.

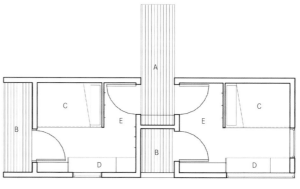

Cabin C floor plan

A. Entry walkway
B. Deck
C. Bed with storage
D. Desk and built-ins
E. Indoor mudroom

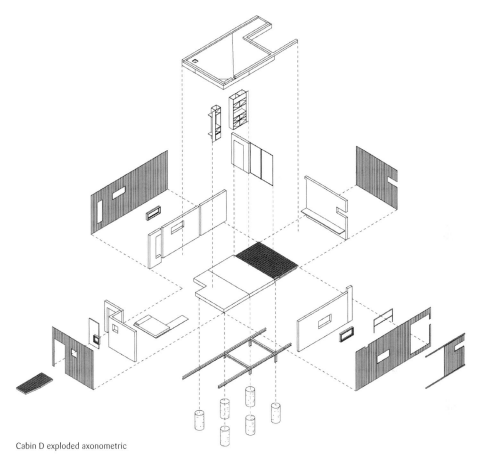

Cabin D exploded axonometric

103

The sustainable approach of the project and the remoteness of the site required that the cabins be prefabricated and assembled on the site.

104

All the materials used on the
exterior and in the interior were
chosen for their durability and
their natural appeal to facilitate the
integration of the cabins into the
natural surroundings.

Cabin D floor plan

A. Entry   D. Bed
B. Indoor mudroom E. Built-in cabinets
C. Deck   F. Desk

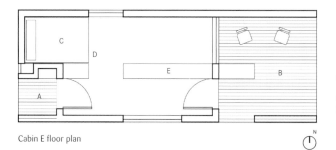

Cabin E floor plan

A. Entry
B. Deck
C. Bed with storage
D. Trundle bed (below)
E. Kitchen island

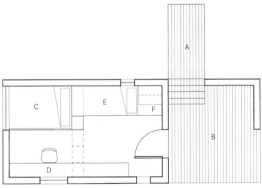

Cabin F floor plan

A. Entry walkway
B. Deck
C. Bed with storage
D. Desk and built-ins
E. Seating/overflow
F. Storage

105

Openings in the walls and passages between modules offer framed views of the immediate landscape.

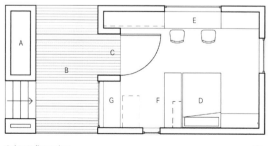

Cabin X floor plan

A. Outdoor storage
B. Deck
C. Entry
D. Bed with storage
E. Desk with built-ins
F. Kitchen
G. Seating

106

Protected outdoor areas were provided to encourage social interaction among users of the cabins.

The Cabin is a wooden structure that stands on top of one of many former concrete bunkers built near the Czech Republic border with Austria. These bunkers were built before World War II as shelters against Nazi troops. There are still thousands of these bunkers left with no actual purpose. Jan Tyrpekl designed a tower that can easily be mounted on or removed from a bunker without affecting the integrity of its construction. Friends, family, and students of architecture participated in the design and construction of the tower. The tower was first constructed off-site, then disassembled and transported to the site, where it was reassembled.

The Cabin

135 sq ft

Jan Tyrpekl

Vratěnín,
Czech Republic

© Antonín Matějovský

Because of the character of the landscape, the design team conceived the tower as dominant vertically. The building has two large windows, one facing east toward the border with Austria and the other offering a view of the nearest village's church tower. The building serves as a shelter for anyone to stay in upon request.

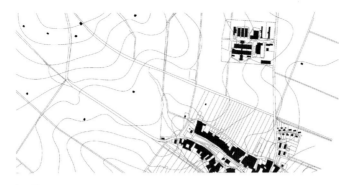

Location map

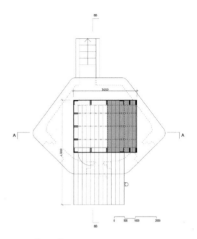

Upper floor plan

North elevation

East elevation

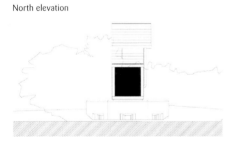

South elevation

West elevation

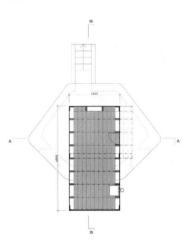

Lower floor plan

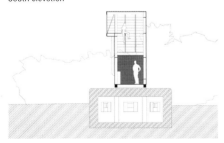

Section A-A

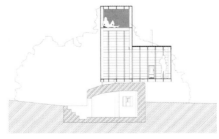

Section B-B

107

The principle of the construction was to minimize the use of material, construction cost, and building time. The building is very simple and can be built by manual labor using only common tools without any technology. The project isn't financed through any donations or grants.

Koto is the Finnish word for *cozy at home*. It is also the name given to the firm formed by design duo Johnathon and Zoë Little. The couple wanted to acknowledge not only the minimal aesthetics of Scandinavian design they have become so attached to but also the Nordic lifestyle and the value of a healthy work-life balance. The design of this small cabin encourages people to connect with nature and embrace outdoor living. Partnering with skilled UK production teams has brought an exceptional level of experience and craftsmanship to the finished product, capitalizing on low energy use and timber-frame buildings.

Koto Cabins

161–430 sq ft

Koto Design

Westward Ho!,
United Kingdom

© Joe Laverty

108

Living small challenges how people think about buildings, from construction to their impact on the environment at every step along the way.

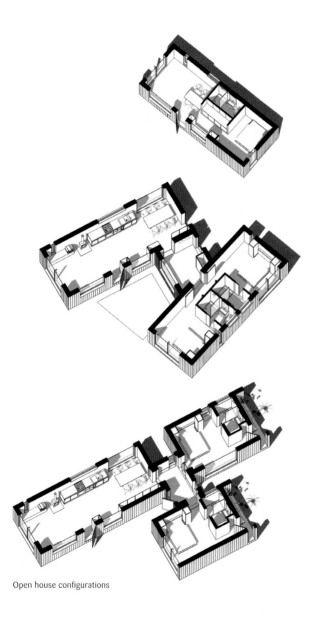

Sauna

Small cabin

Medium cabin

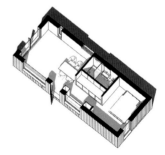

Open house configurations

Large cabin

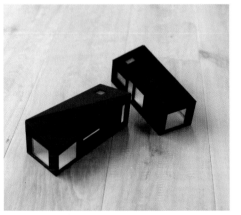

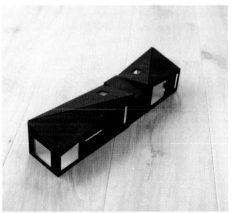

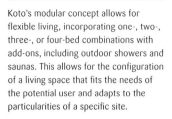

109

Koto's modular concept allows for flexible living, incorporating one-, two-, three-, or four-bed combinations with add-ons, including outdoor showers and saunas. This allows for the configuration of a living space that fits the needs of the potential user and adapts to the particularities of a specific site.

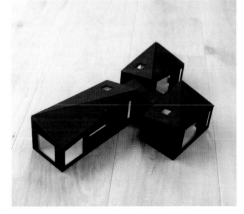

Expansive concealed storage, cozy
nooks, and built-in window seats
maximize floor space and promote
a clean aesthetic while connecting
occupants to the outside world.
Although working within a relatively
small footprint, the tall diagonal ridge
opens up the spaces dramatically.

110

Each bedroom is designed to feel like a private retreat within the landscape, and key pieces of furniture all from Hay have been curated to create a calm, minimal environment. Occupants can enjoy a flexible space to sleep, to relax, and to disconnect.

Klein A45

180 sq ft

Bjarke Ingels Group

Lanesville, Indiana,
United States

© Matthew Carbone

A45 is a cabin prototype designed for Klein, a prefab-housing
company committed to the tiny house lifestyle. The cabin
can be customizable for potential homeowners to purchase,
tailor, and have the tiny house built within four to six months
in any location, for any purpose. The design evolves from
the traditional A-frame cabin, known for its pitched roof and
angled walls, which allow for easy rain run-off and simple
construction. A45 is assembled in modules on site and consists
of 100 percent recyclable materials, including the timber-frame
wall modules and subfloor. The interior reflects a minimal
Nordic abode, prioritizing comfort and design.

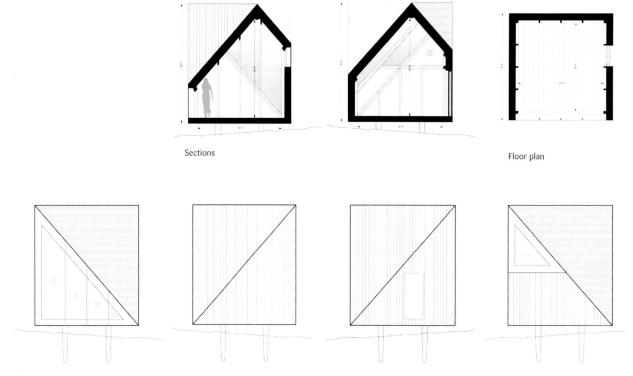

Sections

Floor plan

Elevations

To maximize the qualities of this typical structure, A45 creates more usable floor area by taking a square base and twisting the roof 45 degrees, raising the tiny home to a soaring 13-foot height.

111

The triangular floor-to-ceiling window featuring seven glass pieces allows natural daylight to illuminate the interiors. The structure is slightly elevated from the ground by four concrete piers to give optimal support and allow homeowners to place their tiny house in even the roughest terrains.

The use of exposed timber frame in solid pine, Douglas fir floor, and customizable space-grade insulating natural cork walls bring nature inside the cabin. A Morsø wood-burning stove is nestled in one corner, while off-the-grid equipment is tucked away, out of sight.

112

A petite kitchen is designed by
Københavns Møbelsnedkeri.
The bathroom is made of cedar
wood with fixtures by VOLA.

The architectural challenge for Atelier LAVIT was to create a functional and comfortable hotel room, being faithful to the project's first inspirational vision: a bird's nest. As many customers often define it, ORIGIN is an exceptional cabin, a unique and tailor-made project. A meeting point between poetry and carpentry, the ORIGIN tree house stands out among the centenarian oaks of the Château de Raray forest, as if it has always been part of the scenery.

ORIGIN
Tree House Hotel
248–377 sq ft

Atelier LAVIT

Raray, France

© Marco Lavit

A wooden bridge, thirty feet above the ground, leads guests to the nest. The octagonal plan organizes the space around the oak trunk, incorporating it into the inhabited space.

ORIGIN tree house general overview

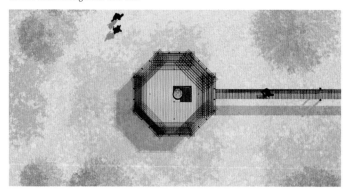

ORIGIN tree house roof plan

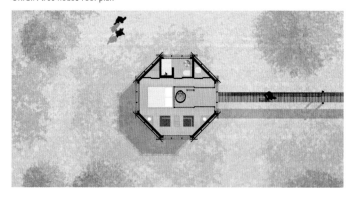

ORIGIN tree house floor plan

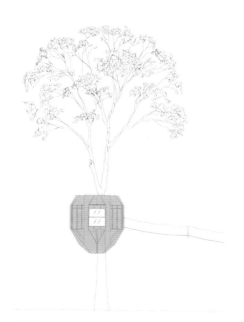

ORIGIN tree house elevation

ORIGIN tree house section A-A

ORIGIN tree house section B-B

ORIGIN tree house section C-C

ORIGIN tree house section D-D

ORIGIN tree house section E-E

The design of the cabin, coupled
with traditional wood construction
techniques, led to a rationalization of
the assembly logic of the branches
collected by the birds to create their
nests.

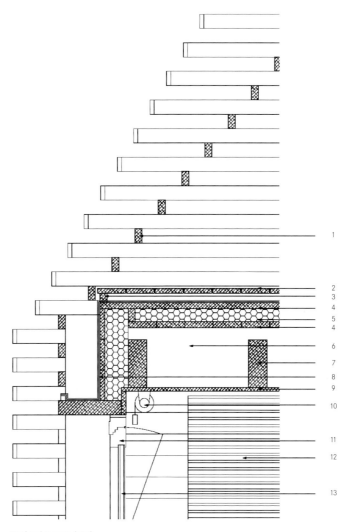

Roof and terrace detail

1. Douglas fir cladding
2. Douglas fir decking
3. Wood subfloor
4. OSB panel
5. Mineral wool insulation
6. Pine beam
7. Pine joist
8. Insulating membrane EPDM
9. Poplar ceiling
10. Blackout shade
11. Reynaers SL38 tilting
    windows
12. Poplar laticework
13. Double glazing

113

The advantage of designing a small space is that details can be resolved at an almost furniture scale.

Once on the patio, a feeling of
protection reigns as in a nest, with an
easy access to the living area through
two large sliding glass doors.

114

An interstitial space between the deck and the tree house adds a layer of protection.

Inside, a cozy, bright, and intimate atmosphere fills the space with large windows that bring the forest in. The walls are clad in poplar, which has a pleasant creamy color and a straight, uniform grain. The smooth, flat interior walls are matched by custom-made furniture that adds to the comfort of this tiny hideaway.

115

The construction method of the tree house is brought to the interior down to the smallest detail, creating slatted surfaces that add texture and depth to the small space.

The GCP Wood Cabin Hotel comprises fourteen small suites distributed around a fishing reserve, on the shore of a lake, floating on the water like rafts, or on piles like palafittes. The imperative for the architect was the absolute symbiosis with the existing landscape and minimal environmental impact. The architectural work blends with the lacustrine environment, taking the tall and swaying reeds as inspiration to form the exterior skin of the cabins. At the same time, the distinct wood buildings also evoke primitive constructions.

GCP Wood Cabin Hotel

248 sq ft

Atelier LAVIT

Sorgues, France

© Marco Lavit

Cabins reflected on the water create
a magical atmosphere that changes
through the seasons.

Master plan

116

Because of the remoteness of the site, the cabins were, for the most part, prefabricated off-site in a workshop. The components were numbered, dismantled, and rebuilt on site within three months. This process reduced production and installation costs.

During the day, the experience inside the suite is a play of light and shadow with the sun filtering through the screens. Random gaps provide abstract glimpses of the vegetation, the lake, and the sky. At sunset, the effect is reversed: immersed in darkness and illuminated only by the moon, the cabins look like lit lanterns, with a golden light emanating through their wooden screens.

117

A variety of plans appeals to a wider audience, who can choose their stay based on location, form, and typology.

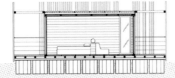

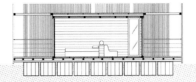

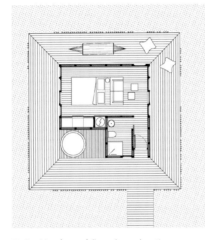

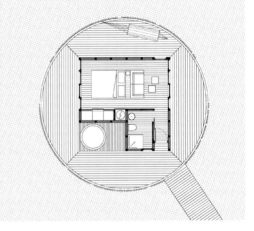

DUO cabin 1 (square) floor plan and section

DUO cabin 2 (circular) floor plan and section

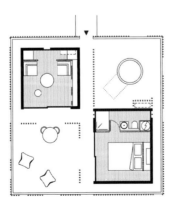

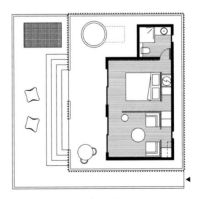

Floating DUO cabin floor plan

DUO cabin on pilotis floor plan

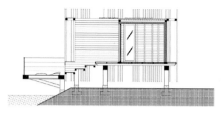

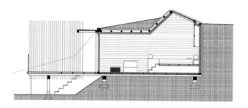

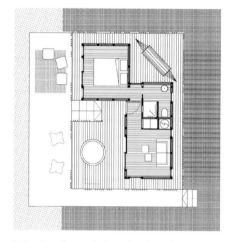

DUO cabin 3 (water edge) on pilotis floor plan and section

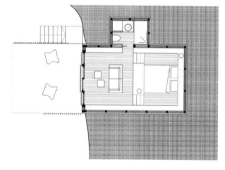

DUO cabin 4 (ground) floor plan and section

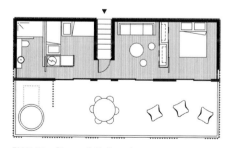

FAMILIAL cabin on pilotis floor plan

118

An appealing constructed form that echoes the surrounding landscape based on a sustainability principle will attract an audience of nature lovers.

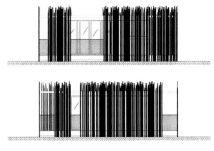

Square cabins southeast elevations

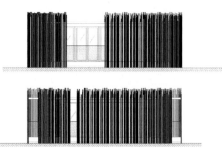

Circular cabins southeast elevations

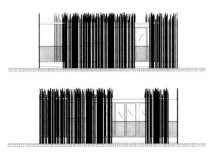

Square cabins northwest elevations

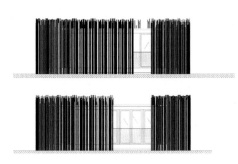

Circular cabins northwest elevations

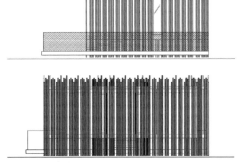

FAMILIAL cabins on piles, northeast elevations

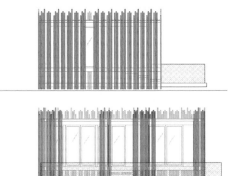

FAMILIAL cabins on piles, southwest elevations

119

A strong architectural language inspired by the natural setting helps integrate architecture into its surroundings.

120

A bed under a skylight is close to
sleeping under the stars, but with
the comfort of a cozy space.

DD26
280 sq ft

DublDom

Volga River, North of Moscow,
Russia

© DublDom

DublDom is a Russian-based design-build company specializing in the production of prefabricated modular houses. Because they are prefabricated, they can be easily transported, and once on the site, they can be assembled in a single day. DublDom offers a line of five different models of varying configurations and sizes ranging between 280 and 1,400 square feet. DD26 is their smallest. Despite its small size, this compact house is provided with the same features that its larger counterparts benefit from: triple glazing, wood doors and windows, wood finishes, integrated wiring and plumbing, and radiant floor heating in the bathroom. DD26 also has water and sewer connections for easy hook-up to local electrical and water supplies.

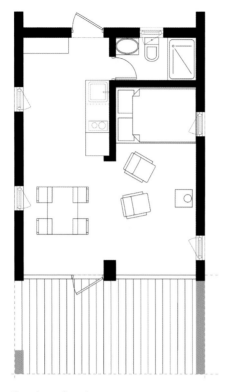

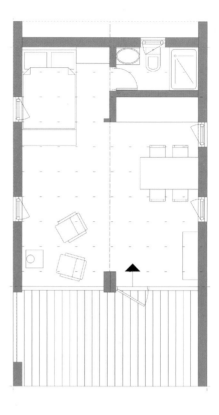

Floor plan configurations

121

The open plan provides onubstructed
views of the river, providing a sense
of expansiveness.

122

The DublDom technology saves resources at all stages of the development and cuts down on construction time. The result is an energy-efficient, eco-friendly building that has a minimal impact on the environment.

123

Perfect for a holiday retreat, this tiny DublDom house has all the warm wood interiors one would expect to find in a cabin in the woods.

124

Floating barges give a sense of
freedom that hardly any other type
of space can provide.

The warm wood of the floating cabin balances out the aquatic environment, providing an earthy element.

DublDom has produced a series of wood-frame prefabricated dwellings in line with its modular principles. The design of these compact dwellings makes them especially suitable for vacation homes and temporary housing. They also offer significant benefits and opportunities when challenged by remote locations. The latest variation is this floating cabin called the DublDom Houseboat. It stands on pontoons on the Volga River, a three-hour drive north of Moscow, where it serves as a guest suite for the Paluba Hotel. As both the houseboat and the pontoon system are modular, larger versions can be produced.

DublDom Houseboat
280 sq ft

DublDom

Volga River, North of Moscow, Russia

© DublDom

The floating cabin is solidly moored to the river edge for stability and easy access from land.

125

Like other DublDom constructions, the floating version comes insulated and wired. Utilities can be planned either for shore connections or for off-grid setup.

The DublDom Houseboat has a shore-built version, which has the same design and floor plan as its floating counterpart. Each has an open living area with a fully glazed wall facing a porch. The bedroom and bathroom are located at the back of this compact home for more privacy.

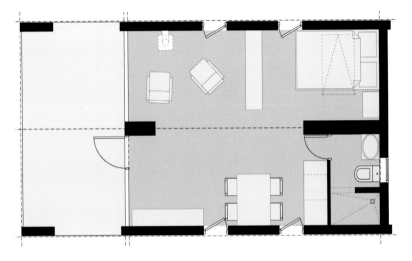

Floor plan

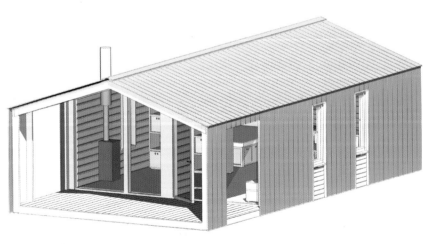

Axonometric view

Windows on all sides of the DubleDom Houseboat invite natural light in, making the home feel inviting. Minimal furnishing and generous storage maximize the use of space.

126

Minimal partitioning allows long
views of the surrounding natural
setting.

The LightHotel served as a beacon for sustainability and ecotourism between 2016 and 2018. One highlight was the Minnesota State Fair at the Eco-Experience, the Minnesota Pollution Control Agency's premier outreach opportunity. The LightHotel's sustainable design elements include its reused and repurposed shipping container shell, its ability to harness solar power, a greywater system, and the fact that it leaves a little-to-light footprint as it moves throughout the Twin Cities. Built by Alchemy Architects and a team of University of the Minnesota architecture students, the LightHotel is an art and architecture project, illustrating the crossroads between staying small and living large.

LightHotel
120 sq ft

Alchemy Architects

Minneapolis-Saint Paul,
Minnesota,
United States

© Alchemy Architects

According to Alchemy's founder, Geoffrey Warner, "the LightHotel is part of an ongoing effort to celebrate and create new paradigms for efficient living." To date, the LightHotel was presented at the Minneapolis Institute of Art (Mia) during the Art of Sustainable Design, the Stone Arch Bridge during Northern Spark, Eaux Claires Art and Music Festival, and the Carleton Artist Lofts.

127

The LightHotel is built for year-round use in Minnesota and features spray foam insulation, triple-paned windows, solar powered HVAC, LED lighting, and hydronic in-floor heating. Its 250-gallon water tank—stored under the queen-size bed— on-demand water heater, and wet room with shower and toilet keep a body happy and fresh. A protected front porch provides a friendly welcome!

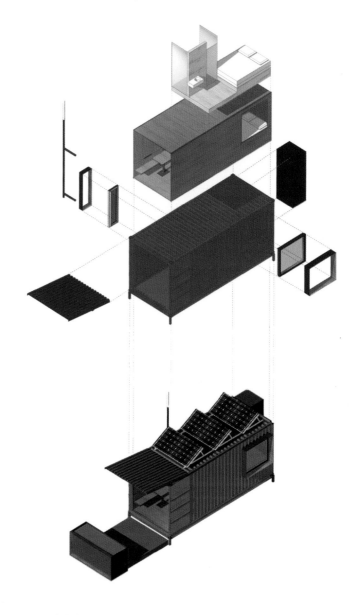

Exploded axonometric

Container

Salvaged container | apertures for light, sight, inputs, and outputs

Thermal

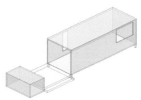

2″ insulated systems box | 4″ spray foam floor | 1″ additional floor | 2″ walls | 4″ ceiling | triple-glazed windows and doors

Power

Thermal floor | pv array | beacon | lighting | television | router/ modem | pv converter | electrical box | city hook-up

Water

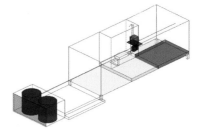

Water pump/pressure tank | city hook-up | sink water storage | shower head | pump/pressure tank | water heater

Waste

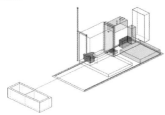

Toilet | wind-powered fan | drain | pump/pressure tank | bio-filter | liquid waste storage | water storage tank

Envelope

Container | front porch | gold leaf window shrouds | triple-paned windows

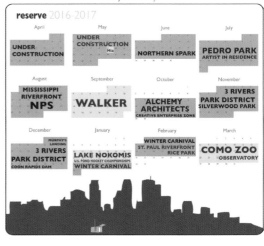

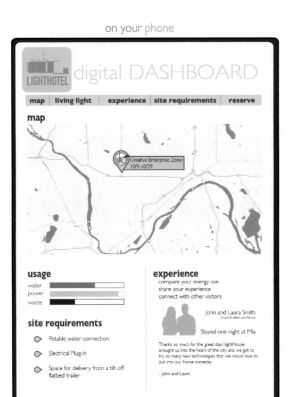

Smart controls

128

The LightHotel sparks community awareness of sustainable design and starts a bigger discussion around living "lighter." LightHotel guests educate themselves on conservation and ecotourism by plugging into an online public digital dashboard that maps water and power usage along with guest experiences.

129

The LightHotel personalizes and celebrates the potential for a more sustainable future in building design. It is both efficient and comfortable while making the most of limited space within the salvaged 8′ x 20′ shipping container.

130

Interesting patterns add a playful
touch to the wood interior, which
conveys a sense of calm and luxury.

Owner Matt White and his crew from Recycling the Past have created an amazing new lodging concept, born from pure wanderlust, an inherent obligation to recycle, and a constant need to create. Reclaimed artifacts acquired during Matt's travels around the globe adorn each "Houze," making the décor one of a kind. Each place is unique, featuring creative design solutions. Flophouzes are designed for the enjoyment of life away from the noise and rushes of the city.

Flophouze Hotel
300 sq ft

Recycling the Past

Round Top, Texas,
United States

© Taylor Prinsen and Flophouze

131

Steel shipping containers are spurring a recycling trend thanks to their durability, adaptability, low cost, and easy stacking, lending to the construction of tiny homes and hotel rooms among other types of habitable spaces.

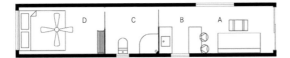

Flophouze I

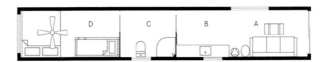

Flophouze IV

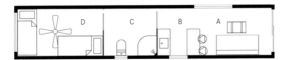

Flophouze II

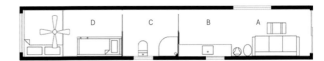

Flophouze V

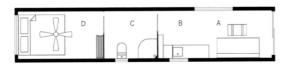

Flophouze III

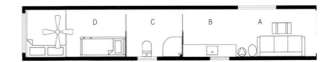

Flophouze VI

A. Living area   C. Bathroom
B. Kitchen   D. Bedroom

132

The simple boxy shape of shipping
containers offers stunning design
opportunities, including infinite
configurations by combining two
or more.

133

The interior of the steel shipping containers can be lined with softer materials to create an inviting atmosphere. The use of recycled finishes such as reclaimed wood reinforces the idea of sustainability.

Whitewashed wood walls and ceiling create a cozy feel. This finish works particularly well in bedrooms, providing a soothing atmosphere.

135

Inside the shipping container, the ceiling height is comparable to that of a typical residential space. This allows for the use of off-the-shelf construction materials and furniture.

Regular plumbing fixtures can easily be installed. Once totally finished and furnished, the interior of a shipping container gives little indication of its previous purpose.

CABN was created to help provide people with a means to disconnect from the craziness we have brought upon ourselves. The Kangaroo Valley cabin is handcrafted with as many local materials as possible, sustainable, eco-friendly, and easy to install. These are major selling points that make the cabin so appealing to those who share CABN's philosophy: "to live, leaving no footprint." Composting toilets, rainwater catchment, and solar power make this tiny home 100 percent off-grid. The cabin is perfect as a second home, a studio, a mini retreat, a holiday home, or a guesthouse.

Arabella CABN
161 sq ft

CABN

Kangaroo Valley,
New South Wales,
Australia

© Newstyle Media

137

The cabin is a sustainable and eco-friendly tiny house. It is set in some of Australia's most stunning and stimulating landscapes, offering an ideal escape completely off-grid.

138

The open character of the cabin is enhanced by the large openings that bring the outdoors in.

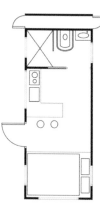

Main floor plan

Sleeping loft plan

The Cornelia Tiny House was conceived as a guesthouse, a writing studio, and a library for children's book author Cornelia Funke. It provides for a peaceful and quiet retreat nestled in an oak forest alongside another structure on the same property. The materials used are just as sturdy as they are full of character. With time, these materials will show an ever-changing patina of shades and textures that progressively blend with the surrounding natural settings. The interior isn't fitted for long-term accommodation but offers, even for a short time, a reassuring sense of harmony and connection with nature, a sense that only spaces with such human proportions and intimate relationship with its immediate context can give.

Cornelia Tiny House
250 sq ft

New Frontier Tiny Homes

Malibu, California,
United States

© StudiObuell Photography

The Cornelia Tiny House is designed from a simple floor plan to include a writing studio, a king-size bedroom with a 270-degree view, a living room, a kitchenette, and a half bathroom. At twenty-four feet long and eight and a half feet wide, the trailer was not designed for full-time living but can be occupied both on- or off-grid.

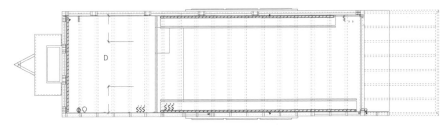

Upper level floor plan

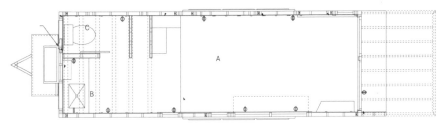

A. Great room/writing studio
B. Kitchen
C. Water closet
D. Loft

Lower level floor plan

139

Cabin design generally prioritizes the optimization of usable space within a reduced footprint, while encouraging the use of outdoor space.

Constructed using only the highest quality materials and craftsmanship, the Cornelia Tiny House was built the New Frontier way, incorporating beautiful rustic finishes. Corrugated metal cladding, custom wood stains on maple siding, and reclaimed hardwood flooring integrate the Tiny House into its natural setting.

140

A built-in desk along one side of the trailer can be folded down, adding some extra space to the limited floor area. Minimal furniture provides for the bare-essential commodities.

141

Windows around the loft bed make the tight space feel less confined and more comfortable while giving the impression of sleeping outdoors, but with the comfort and coziness of a protected space.

Custom cedar library shelves were designed to house the author's book collection. The trailer features glass doors and windows on all sides so that natural light can pour into the interior. The clerestory windows give the impression that the ceiling is higher than it actually is.

Even tiny kitchens can have style, offering the opportunity to apply design ingenuity to small proportions.

What a small space lacks in floor area, it can make up for in charm. Color and materials can provide a small space with zest without compromising its functionality.

The owner sought to replace an existing single car garage on their property with a living unit to provide permanent accommodations for a retired parent. As a result, the Kerns Micro-House was devised as an accessory dwelling unit, meeting the City of Portland's stringent design standards and a sympathetic response to the concerns with increasing density in the area. The Kern Micro-House was also conceived as an inhabitable part of the surrounding natural setting, adding to the architectural character of the building.

Kerns Micro-House
250 sq ft

Fieldwork Design & Architecture

Portland, Oregon, United States

© Dana Klein, Polara

144

The exterior skin is formed by a local fir board and batten system, which was prototyped in the Fieldwork shop and detailed at a furniture scale. The minimalist interior includes custom Oregon white oak furniture and cabinetry enhanced by generous natural lighting.

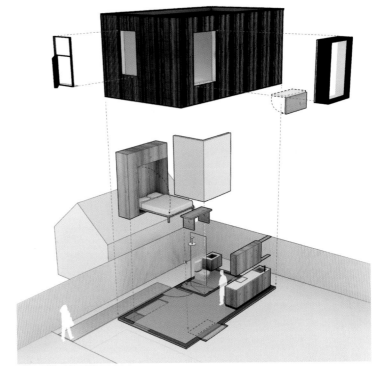

Exploded axonometric

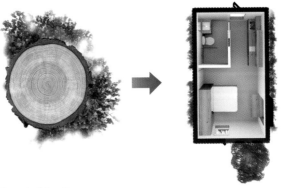

Conceptual diagram

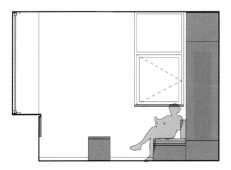

Couch and coffee table

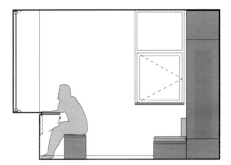

Desk

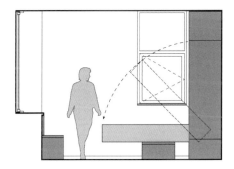

Murphy bed

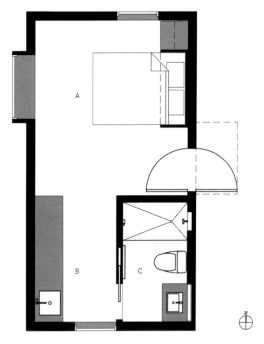

Floor plan

A. Living and sleeping
B. Kitchen
C. Bathroom

145

Innovative solutions include a drawer that doubles as a nightstand when extended, a coffee table that offers itself as a bench for a fold-out window desk, and a Murphy bed/ storage unit. The custom furniture was designed and buit to be adaptive and flexible, maximizing space and utility.

146

The minimalistic interior design focuses on the chromatic, tactile, and decorative character of the materials used.

Plús Hús

320 sq ft

Minarc

Santa Monica, California,
United States

© Art Gray Photography

Plús Hús—Icelandic for *plus house*—is an innovative accessory
dwelling unit (ADU) designed by world-renowned environmentally
conscious architectural design firm Minarc. Plús Hús responds to
the Los Angeles law changes that expand usage options for ADUs
installed in the backyards of single family homes. Plús Hús makes
adding an attractive private space to one's property not only more
affordable and environmentally responsible than existing ADU
options but also extremely simple. It is a 16' x 20' customizable
structure that mixes Minarc's minimalist nordic-style aesthetic with
an energy efficient mnmMOD panel system. A Plús Hús can serve
as a guesthouse, home office, art studio, or low-maintenance
Airbnb rental.

147

There are three models of Plús Hús: the "Plús Hús Open," with three walls and a sliding glass door; the "Plús Hús Open+," which includes a bathroom; and the "Plús Hús Full," which, in addition to a bathroom, features a kitchen along the back wall.

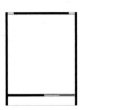

Plús Hús Open floor plan

Plús Hús Open+ floor plan

Plús Hús Full floor plan

Front elevation

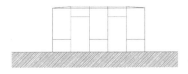

Side elevation

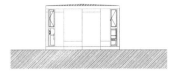

Rear elevation

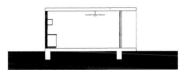

Sections

A. Kitchen
B. Covered porch
C. Bathroom

148

The use of the same finish material on all the surfaces creates a sense of continuous homogeneity that brings serenity and comfort into the space.

Lake Harriet Loft

380 sq ft

Christopher Strom Architects

Minneapolis, Minnesota,
United States

© Alyssa Lee Photography

The scope of the project included a new guest dwelling
connected to an existing home by a new elevated deck. A new
city zoning ordinance allowed this classification of accessory
dwelling unit to be built on a single-family parcel already
containing a primary residence. The site parameters were
challenging; Minneapolis rules for accessory dwellings require a
twenty-foot separation from the primary residence. A variance
was granted to build within seven feet because an existing
foundation was used from an existing outbuilding. Program
goals included the creation of an independent accommodation
for visiting friends and relatives. Potentially, the dwelling had to
be appealing enough for Airbnb rental income.

The heft and scale of a bridge and other historic remnants are strong contextual forces. The simple formal language of the new building recognizes the importance of being a complementary neighbor within this context.

The project is sited at the intersection of an abandoned streetcar line and prominent boulevard bridge. It is visible from vehicles and heavy pedestrian traffic.

Remnant path of streetcar line   ++++++++

Major boulevard

Pedestrian path

Convergence of site forces

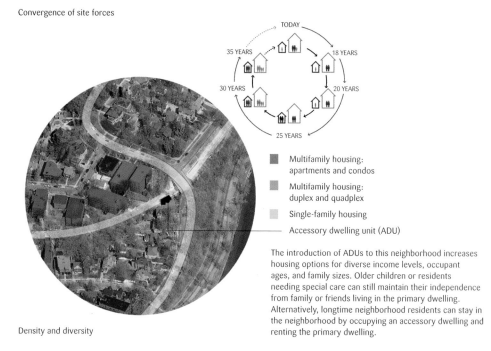

Multifamily housing: apartments and condos

Multifamily housing: duplex and quadplex

Single-family housing

Accessory dwelling unit (ADU)

The introduction of ADUs to this neighborhood increases housing options for diverse income levels, occupant ages, and family sizes. Older children or residents needing special care can still maintain their independence from family or friends living in the primary dwelling. Alternatively, longtime neighborhood residents can stay in the neighborhood by occupying an accessory dwelling and renting the primary dwelling.

Density and diversity

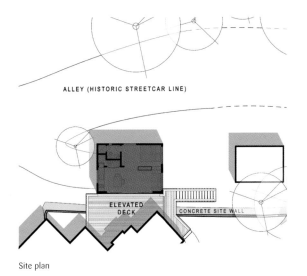

ALLEY (HISTORIC STREETCAR LINE)

ELEVATED DECK

CONCRETE SITE WALL

Site plan

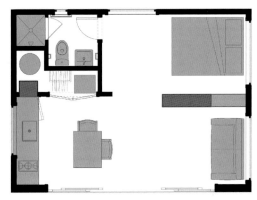

Floor plan

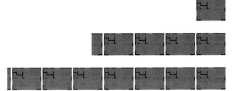

380 sq ft   Project footprint

1660 sq ft   Average American house in 1973*

2687 sq ft   Average American house in 2015*

*According to the Census Bureau annual report *2016 Characteristics of New Housing*; statistics are for newly constructed single-family homes.

All interior spaces are connected to the exterior with large openings that relate to framed views, visual connections, or physical access. Views on all four sides make the tiny space seem larger. Views include the tree canopy, neighborhood vistas, and the historic streetcar bridge.

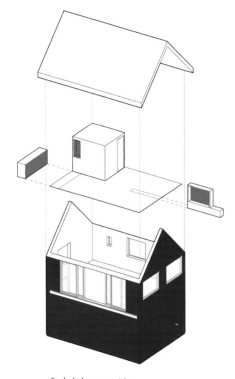

Exploded axonometric

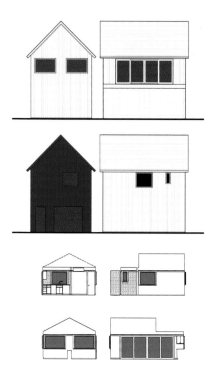

Exterior and interior elevations

An elevated deck spans the remains of a municipal retaining wall to connect the dwelling to the primary residence. The accessory dwelling takes advantage of this elevated deck with views for outdoor entertainment, while parking is housed in the lower level, which is connected to the alley.

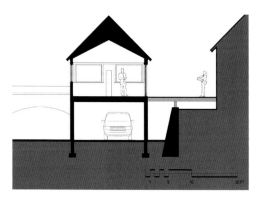

Section

The aesthetic "spirit" of the new building was found in photos of colorful Norwegian fishing villages, a complementary counterpoint to the existing context. The red vertical siding unifies the exterior volume and its iconic vertical proportions.

A monochromatic palette of walls, trim, and ceiling increases the perceived volume. Built-in cabinetry organizes distinct spatial zones and uses color to create focal points. A storage and utility core consolidates elements that obstruct views.

DIRECTORY

A+B Kasha Designs
Paris, France
www.abkasha.com

A Little Design
Taipei, Taiwan
www.facebook.com/Design.A.Little/

Alchemy Architects
Saint Paul, Minnesota, United States
www.weehouse.com

Architecture Workshop
Brooklyn, New York, United States
Paris, France
www.aw-pc.com

Atelier Daaa
Paris, France
www.atelierdaaa.com

Atelier LAVIT
Paris, France
www.atelier-lavit.com

Atelier Wilda
Vannes, France
www.wilda.fr

Bjarke Ingels Group
Copenhagen, Denmark
London, United Kingdom
Brooklyn, New York, United States
www.big.dk

Black & Milk
London, United Kingdom
www.blackandmilk.co.uk

B.L.U.E. Architecture Studio
Beijing, People's Republic of China
www.b-l-u-e.net

Brad Swartz Architects
Darlinghurst, New South Wales, Australia
www.bradswartz.com.au

CABN
Adelaide, South Australia, Australia
www.cabn.life

Casa 100
São Paulo, Brazil
www.casa100.com.br

Catseye Bay
Surry Hills, New South Wales, Australia
www.catseyebay.com

Christopher Strom Architects
Saint Louis Park, Minnesota, United States
www.christopherstrom.com

Colorado Building Workshop
Denver, Colorado, United States
www.coloradobuildingworkshop
.cudenvercap.org

DesignBuildBLUFF
Salt Lake City, Utah, United States
www.designbuildbluff.org

DublDom
Moscow, Russia
www.dubldom.com/en

Elie Metni
Beirut, Lebanon
www.eliemetni.com

Fieldwork Design & Architecture
Portland, Oregon, United States
www.fieldworkdesign.net

FREAKS Architecture
Paris, France
www.freaksarchitecture.com

Gnocchi+Danesi Architects
Milan, Italy
www.themountainrefuge.com

Graham Hill/LifeEdited
New York City, New York, United States
www.lifeedited.com

Jan Tyrpekl
Prague, Czech Republic
www.tyrpekl.wixsite.com/portfolio

Koto Design
Bideford, United Kingdom
www.kotodesign.co.uk

LLABB
Genoa, Italy
www.llabb.eu

Lorena Troncoso-Valencia
Concepción, Chile
www.lorenatroncoso.cl

Lund Hagem
Oslo, Norway
www.lundhagem.no

Maguire + Devine Architects
Hobart, Tasmania
www.maguiredevine.com.au

Michael K Chen Architecture/MKCA
New York City, New York, United States
www.mkca.com

Minarc
Santa Monica, California, United States
www.minarc.com

nARCHITECTS
Brooklyn, New York, United States
www.narchitects.com

New Frontier Tiny Homes
Nashville, Tennessee, United States
www.newfrontiertinyhomes.com

Out of the Valley
Exeter, United Kingdom
www.outofthevalley.co.uk

Phoebe Sayswow Architects
Taipei, Taiwan
www.phoebesayswow.com

PLANAIR
Milan, Italy
www.planairstudio.com

Recycling the Past
Barnegat, New Jersey, United States
www.recyclingthepast.com

Renato Arrigo
Messina, Italy
www.renatoarrigo.com

Reverse Architecture
Somerville, Massachusetts, United States
www.reversearchitecture.com

Richardson Architects
Mill Valley, California, United States
www.richardsonarchitects.com

Ruetemple
Moscow, Russia
www.ruetemple.ru

Rupert McKelvie
Exeter, United Kingdom
www.rupertmckelvie.com

Silvia Allori
Milan, Italy
www.silviaallori.it

Studio Prineas
Rushcutters Bay, New South Wales,
Australia
www.architectprineas.com.au

Szymon Hanczar
Wroclaw, Poland
www.hanczar.com

Taylored Architecture
Clayton, New York, United States
www.tayloredarch.com

Tsai Design
Richmond, Victoria, Australia
www.tsaidesign.com.au

University of Colorado Denver
Denver, Colorado, United States
www.ucdenver.edu

Vertebrae Architecture
Los Angeles, California, United States
www.vertebraela.com

YCL Studio
Vilnius, Lithuania
www.ycl.lt